WHICH BUSINESS?

WHICH BUSINESS?

Tested Ideas for Profitable Enterprises

SECOND EDITION

Stephen Halliday

KOGAN
PAGE

This book is dedicated to those I love and those from whom I've learned.

Copyright © Stephen Halliday 1987, 1990

All rights reserved. No reproduction, copy or transmission of this publication may be made without written permission.

No paragraph of this publication may be reproduced, copied or transmitted save with written permission or in accordance with the provisions of the Copyright Act 1956 (as amended), or under the terms of any licence permitting limited copying issued by the Copyright Licensing Agency, 7 Ridgmount Street, London WC1E 7AE.

Any person who does any unauthorised act in relation to this publication may be liable to criminal prosecution and civil claims for damages.

First published in Great Britain in 1987 by
Kogan Page Limited,
120 Pentonville Road,
London N1 9JN.
Second edition 1990.

British Library Cataloguing in Publication Data
A CIP record for this book is available from the British Library.

ISBN 0-7494-0075-7
ISBN 0-7494-0076-5 Pbk

Typeset by Selectmove Ltd, London
Printed and bound in Great Britain by
Richard Clay, Bungay

Contents

Introduction

In 1983, while I was working as a lecturer in marketing at The Bucking-hamshire College, my wife Jane and I started our own business, based on a profitable hobby of Jane's which she had practised for about eight years. In 1984 I was asked by my colleagues to prepare and conduct a course on small business operations for students of the College. This is an option within the Business and Technician Education Council's HND in Business and Finance. The option started in September 1984 and has proved very popular with students.

My first task with each group of students is to help them develop ideas which will form a suitable basis for a small business. Some produce ideas in which they are genuinely interested and which lend themselves to a small business format. Examples have been a driving school, a gardening service, a knitting shop and a second-hand TV hire business – all ideas which were well thought out and carefully developed.

Other students submit ideas which are much less promising, usually because they lack the experience or substantial capital required to make them work; occasionally because the competitive situation is forbidding. Some students confess that they are looking for ideas and profess a strong desire to start their own businesses, possibly because they come from areas of high unemployment where shortage of jobs makes it hard to find work even for someone with an HND in Business and Finance.

I found that I was able to offer little help to the groups with no ideas or unsuitable ideas. I could question them about the possibility of developing their hobbies into businesses and offer some personal opinions. I felt that I should be able to do more so I set about surveying the large and growing field of small firms and job creation literature in order to remedy this deficiency. I met with little success. Finally, my enquiries took me to Business In The Community (BIC), an organisation sponsored and funded by large companies. Among other activities BIC promotes the Enterprise Agency Network in the UK. Enterprise agencies are concerned with helping small firms to start up and expand. Further information about them is given in Chapter 9.

At Business In The Community, I met Alex Bryce, marketing adviser, who told me that he was aware of shortcomings in the field of idea generation and that BIC would be interested in any research into the subject. I learned that many enterprise agencies are approached by would-be entrepreneurs who wish to start businesses, often with redundancy money, but who lack suitable ideas.

For example, some people who are made redundant with large sums of money after many years of working for a large organisation are fatally attracted by what they perceive as the romantic notion of purchasing a busy little village shop in the area in which they have spent their summer holidays for many years. They overlook the fact that the shop is only busy in summer because of holiday-makers like themselves. The permanent residents of the area make most of their purchases from a hypermarket in the nearby town to which they drive in their hatchbacks once a week, leaving the village shopkeeper to exist on occasional emergency purchases. They also overlook the fact that, in the grocery business, to be small is to be fatally weak. Large organisations like Tesco and Sainsbury's can purchase their supplies from manufacturers on terms which are far more attractive than those available to the small shopkeeper whose prices are thus rendered hopelessly uncompetitive.

Enterprise agencies who were approached by people with unsuitable ideas of this kind could point out the weaknesses but were in no position to suggest more promising lines of enquiry.

Since 1986 I have been continuously engaged in research designed to answer one question. How can the person who wishes to start his or her own business be guided towards business ideas which have a better than even chance of success? While to be small is to be weak in some sectors, such as grocery retailing, there are many other markets in which large-scale operation is much less relevant to success. For example, in the selling of books and newspapers certain peculiarities of these markets (which are described in Chapter 2) mean that small-scale operations are far less of a problem. In other markets, notably the rapidly expanding services sector, flexibility and low overheads offered by the small business may actually confer advantages.

The main purpose of this book, therefore, is to help people to find those market opportunities in which being small is either an advantage or, at the very least, not a disadvantage.

Chapter 1 briefly summarises the main sources of business ideas and makes some initial judgements on their suitability. The chapters which follow go into these in more detail. Chapter 2 makes use of government statistics to identify those sectors of the economy which offer *promising opportunities* for small businesses.

Chapter 3 looks at *ways of bringing together* people who have ideas and those who have resources. For example, you may have experience of selling, administration, production, engineering or some other skill which is needed by an entrepreneur who has an idea but lacks the experience or resources to put that idea into practice. Many organisations now exist to bring together those who have ideas and those who have resources – such as skills or money – which are needed to create a viable business.

Chapter 4, *Licensing Opportunities*, looks at opportunities in the technical field. There are hundreds of opportunities to take licences to manufacture and/or market products which have been developed by companies which are unable to undertake the operation themselves. Such licensing opportunities may be suitable either for start-up businesses or, more commonly, for existing small businesses wishing to diversify their product range.

Chapter 5 covers the activities of the *idea sellers*. These are organisations which offer for sale 'off the peg' business ideas which usually claim to make a great deal of money for people who take them on. These claims are not always true! The chapter introduces some of the organisations in the field and gives advice on how to evaluate the more extravagant claims.

By the time you reach the end of Chapter 5, you should know how to set about finding suitable ideas and draw up a short-list suitable for you. Your next step is to undertake some simple, cost-effective market research which will enable you to evaluate the ideas. Chapter 6 tells you where you can find information which will help you to undertake such *market research* at little or no cost to yourself. Many people go into business by purchasing an existing organisation – a shop, a restaurant, a small manufacturing or service business for example. In this case, the first question that is asked is, 'How much does it cost to buy such a business?' Chapter 7 gives examples of the *prices* which are currently being asked for a number of different types of business. It also gives an indication of the level of sales and gross profit achieved by each.

Chapter 8 is intended as an introduction to *market research methods*. It shows how you can make use of the sources of information in Chapter 6 to research an idea on your short-list. A few pounds and a few hours spent researching an idea can save much heartache and cost later. Chapter 9 looks at *help for small business*: the many organisations which now exist to help businesses in general and small enterprises in particular. I have briefly described the activities of the main schemes in this field and give addresses and telephone numbers from which you can obtain further information. This chapter also includes an up-to-date list of enterprise agencies.

Finally, Chapter 10, *Ideas in Action*, describes 14 business ideas which are currently being operated successfully and profitably by other people and appear to have opportunities for further development. Some of them are described in detail and illustrated by a case study. Others are described in broad outline. I have tried to include ideas which represent a wide variety of skills, knowledge and experience but which do not require much start-up capital. At the very least I hope they will help to get you thinking along positive lines in order to develop your own business idea.

Acknowledgements

Many people have helped me with the writing of this book. I am particularly indebted to three people and one organisation for their helpfulness and patience. Without the encouragement and advice of Alex Bryce of Business In The Community, I would never have undertaken the project. Mrs Pamela Henson of Lakey & Co business transfer agents, went to a great deal of trouble to provide the information on the costs of buying an existing business as described in Chapter 7. Sue Romeril, my long-suffering typist, produced the typescript much more quickly than I deserved. Finally, I am indebted to the staff of the Salon Permanent des Idées d'Affaires for discussing with me, in my inadequate French, a wide range of services and ideas that they offer to would-be entrepreneurs. In return, I hope I have done justice to their activities in Chapter 5.

Stephen Halliday

CHAPTER 1

Finding the Right Idea

Market opportunities

In which markets do small businesses have the best chance of prospering? An analysis of government statistics helps us to identify those market sectors in which *small* firms are well established. The information is described and analysed in more detail in Chapter 2.

Government interest in the small business sector dates from 1969 when the Secretary of State for Trade and Industry, concerned at the apparent decline in the small firms sector, commissioned a report on the subject under the Chairmanship of Professor John Bolton. The report was published in 1971 and concluded that 'The small firms sector is in a state of long-term decline both in size and in its share of economic activity.' Nevertheless, the Bolton Report, as it became known, also concluded that small firms (which it defined as having fewer than 200 employees) had a very important part to play in the modern economy in providing competition and innovation and in creating jobs. It therefore recommended a number of measures to revive the small firms sector.

Since 1971 there has been a steady and sometimes dramatic recovery in the numbers and fortunes of small firms. This revival has been partly caused by the adoption of the measures proposed by the Bolton Report, such as the establishment of the Small Firms Service which, along with the many other schemes designed to promote small firms, is described in Chapter 9. The revival has also been due to the rapid growth of the services sector of the economy which includes many activities suited to the smaller firm. These are analysed in more detail in Chapter 2.

One way of measuring the growth in the number of small firms is to analyse VAT registrations. As soon as a business achieves VAT-rated sales of £23,600 per annum (tax year 1989–90), its owner is obliged to register as a VAT trader. The vast majority registering are small organisations so the figures give an indication of the trends in the size of the UK small business sector. In the period 1980–88 there was a dramatic increase in the number of businesses registered as can be seen from the following figures:

Businesses registered at start of 1980	Businesses registered at end of 1988	Increase	Percentage Increase
1,289,000	1,574,000	285,000	+22

These figures take account of de-registrations (ie businesses closing down or falling below the VAT threshold) so the figure is a real increase. Moreover, the trend has been gathering pace. In the most recent year for which figures are available, 1988, the number of businesses registered increased by 64,000, or 1230 a week. This is the largest annual increase registered in the period concerned. We can analyse the figures in greater detail by sector and from this analysis it is evident that above average growth is coming from fields which are traditionally associated with small business:

Sector	Businesses registered at start of 1980	Businesses registered at end of 1988	Percentage increase
Construction industry	180,900	243,500	+34.6
Finance, property and professional services	79,000	128,200	+62
Other services	126,000	225,500	+79

The construction and service sectors are strongly associated with small business activity and it is clear from the figures that these businesses are increasing in number more rapidly than the average.

Even so, in Great Britain, small firms still account for a smaller proportion of employment than is the case with many of our foreign competitors. In Britain, firms with fewer than 200 employees account for a little over 35 per cent of private sector employment whereas in the USA the figure is closer to 40 per cent. In Japan, where small firms play a vital role in a dynamic economy as suppliers of components to giant industrial corporations, the figure is over 60 per cent. We may conclude, therefore, that there is plenty of room for further growth in the number of small firms in Britain and in the jobs that they create.

The markets which emerge from the statistics as being the most promising for small enterprises are summarised in the list below. More detailed information is to be found in Chapter 2. For the convenience of the reader this analysis has been broken down into four sectors: manufacturing, retailing, catering and service industries.

There are many definitions of a small business. As we have seen, the Bolton Report took as its ceiling 200 employees, though by most people's standards this would be regarded as a business of substantial size. I have therefore adopted more modest figures. For example, when analysing businesses by the number of employees I have concentrated on those which have fewer than ten, or at the most 20 employees. Likewise, I have tried where possible to concentrate on businesses whose turnover is in the range £23,600 to £100,000 per annum. It is not feasible to include a detailed analysis of firms whose turnover falls below £23,600 since very few of them are registered for VAT and therefore they do not appear in published statistics. It is estimated that about 60 per cent of all businesses have a turnover between £23,600 and £100,000 but this figure is significantly exceeded in some sectors and this can give us an indication of the sectors in which small businesses are well established. The main ones are as follows:

- 67 per cent of **construction businesses** fall in this category. The construction industry is one in which it has traditionally been easy to set up with some skill and a little capital. However, it should also be observed that bankruptcy levels are very high, often due to inexperienced management overextending itself.

- 65 per cent of businesses categorised as **finance, professional services** and **property** are in this turnover category. This rather broad heading includes insurance brokers, dentists, vets, surveyors, architects and other professional people.

- 66 per cent of **catering** businesses. This is not surprising when one considers the wide range of independent and franchised catering outlets, particularly in the fast food sector.

- 67 per cent of **business services**. For example, advertising agencies, market research, contract cleaning office services, duplicating etc. These are among the most rapidly growing sectors of the economy.

- 74 per cent of **other services**. Hairdressing, launderettes, shoe repairs, pop groups etc.

A more detailed analysis of these categories is to be found in the *Standard Industrial Classification (SIC)* available in most good public libraries. Further details are also given in Chapter 2.

Manufacturing

Small firms are well established in markets which offer small niches not large enough to interest big companies. For example, small units account for a high proportion of jobs in several specialist sectors of the **engineering** and **metal working** business. I was more surprised to note that they account for a surprisingly large proportion of jobs in parts of the food industry, notably **bread and flour confectionery** (this does not include high street bakers) and ice-cream. Further research suggests that these small organisations, usually employing fewer than ten people, are established at the top end of the market where short production runs of high quality products, often made without additives and colourings, command a high price and put a premium on flexible operation and local small-scale distribution. This process has no doubt been helped by the fact that some large companies have scaled down their operations in some markets. A few years ago one of the major bakery companies decided to withdraw from the market because the demand for mass-produced products was declining.

Thus, evidence of big companies rationalising their operations or withdrawing from a market should be scanned for newly created 'opportunity gaps' which can be suitable for exploitation by small firms. For example, rationalisation by firms like Courtaulds in the textile industry has not only been accompanied by growth in imports. It has also left behind gaps in product ranges which some retailers have found difficult to fill, particularly in high quality designer fabrics, and there is some evidence of small operators emerging to meet this demand. This is further reflected in the fact that a high proportion of jobs in the manufacture of women's and girls' clothing is to be found in units employing fewer than ten people.

Timber trades are another group which show evidence of potential for small firms. The production of high quality furniture and fittings for shops and offices are two fields in which units employing small numbers of people account for a high proportion of jobs. In the case of shopfitting, this is no doubt a reflection of the fact that a very high proportion of retailers are independent and these seek tailor-made or adapted units for the wide variety of sizes and types of shop that exist and which may not be suitable for the standardised fittings of the multiple retailers. Finally, small firms are well established in the **printing and publishing of books and periodicals**. This is another market in which small production runs are frequently required because of the multitude of publications available and where the flexibility and speed of a small organisation may therefore be an advantage.

Retailing

An analysis of the available information shows that long, unsocial hours are one of the ingredients for success among small retailers. Thus, **confectioners, tobacconists** and **newsagents, greengrocers** and **florists** do well as independent traders.

A second feature which helps to protect the small trader is an element of price protection through resale price maintenance – **bookshops** and **newsagents**. A high degree of product differentiation (**gift shops, china, bridalware, glassware, jewellery** and **greetings cards**) is another.

Specialist knowledge of complex products (**antiques, camping equipment, garden products, books** and **cycles**) is of importance, since the customer is likely to depend upon the retailer for advice on his or her purchases. This is more likely to be found in an independent shop with a committed and knowledgeable owner than in one of the large chains, many of whose staff are probably part time.

Finally, after-sales service (**soft furnishings, hire and repair businesses**) can give the flexible small retailer a competitive advantage. For further details on the above see Chapter 2.

It is possible to find market segments which are unattractive to the large operators and thus leave an opportunity gap for small retailers. Some neighbourhood grocers have managed to survive by offering a delivery service to elderly or housebound customers. This involves extra hours of work for the owner but gives him a competitive advantage over cut-price supermarkets which do not offer this service. Another strategy successfully adopted by some small food shops has been to turn themselves into **convenience stores**. A convenience store is, generally speaking, a combination of a newsagent and a grocer, and further characterised by long opening hours. They depend for their success upon a large number of customers making small purchases – a newspaper, a packet of cigarettes and a carton of milk, for example. They are able to charge higher margins for the convenience.

Another field in which some small retailers are doing well is **TV hire**. A few years ago the larger chains started to close branches and consolidate their activities in a static market. This left some small to medium-sized towns without a branch of their own and thus created an opportunity for independents to emphasise their local availability and prompt service, thereby gaining business at the expense of the larger operators.

This is another example of a small business 'opportunity gap' following rationalisation by a large firm. Moreover, many large TV hire firms will not hire sets to certain categories of the population. These vary, but include people living in furnished accommodation, those with bankruptcy orders outstanding and those on social security who have not previously hired a TV. Some small operators specialise in hiring reconditioned second-hand colour sets to these groups, having bought the sets in working order from the chains for as little as £20 to £25 each.

The effects of the uniform business rate will be felt by retailers. Those in the south of England who sell fixed price goods are particularly at risk. The high interest rate affects everybody in business, but especially shops selling household goods and furnishings.

Catering

The catering trade was one of the fastest growing markets in the 1980s. In the period 1980–86 the number of outlets increased by over 9 per cent and their turnover increased by nearly 70 per cent. Moreover, the most rapid growth of all was in **take-aways**, in which small businesses are particularly well represented. During the period concerned, the number of outlets increased by 25 per cent and their turnover by a phenomenal 120 per cent. This growth is partly fed by the parallel development of the service sector which we observed earlier. An increasing proportion of the population works in small offices and service businesses which are without cantccns. Sandwich bars and similar establishments have sprung up to meet their needs. Apart from independent operators, there are also many franchise operations in the fast food sector which offer opportunities to franchisees, though substantial capital is often required to take up one of these franchises. More information on franchising is to be found in Chapter 3.

Contract catering is also expanding rapidly with a growth of 44 per cent in the number of businesses and 106 per cent in their turnover. Although there are several large firms in this sector, many small operators prosper in specialist fields such as executive lunches and high quality meals for companies who wish to entertain customers. Further information on such operations is given in Chapter 10.

Services

It is universally accepted that the service sector of our economy is one that is growing very rapidly but it is also notoriously difficult to analyse in any detail. The reason lies in the exceptionally wide variety of service businesses that exist: hairdressers, accountants, plumbers and chartered surveyors are all classified as services but that is about all they have in common!

However, even with these constraints one can discern some patterns in the service sector. The number of jobs classified as **professional business services** increased by 31 per cent in the period 1982–87 compared with a growth of less than 2 per cent in the economy as a whole. Professional business services include accountants, surveyors, architects and other qualified people. The growth is much more rapid in **other business services**, where over the same period, the growth was 66 per cent. There are clearly plenty of opportunities in this field which includes secretarial services, contract cleaning, advertising and market research. For further details see Chapter 2.

Occasionally, we learn of opportunity gaps from our experience. Dyno-

Rod (now a multinational franchise organisation) was started by a citizen of New York who had difficulty in finding a plumber to clear his blocked drain. He bought the necessary equipment, cleared the drain himself and realised that others must need the service as well. This is not the only new business to have been spawned by the shortcomings of the plumbing trade! In 1982, a citizen of Munich started a business called 'The Dripping Tap' to carry out very simple plumbing repairs in which the established plumbing firms were not interested. He earns a good living, changing washers and performing other simple plumbing jobs. His arrival was welcomed by the big firms who now refer enquiries to him, as he does to them when he is offered a job he can't handle.

Any service where you have difficulties in finding a suitable supplier for yourself is worth investigating. For example, a highly successful dress hire business was started by two ladies who had difficulty hiring evening dresses to attend a ball at their sons' school. This has also become a successful franchise operation and is referred to in Chapter 10.

Business opportunities presented by changes in the population

Future changes in the structure of the population can be predicted with some confidence. This technique is widely used by large corporations to predict the future of their markets and to develop appropriate strategies, but it can also be used by small firms who are seeking opportunities. For example, the resident population of the United Kingdom is expected to increase by 3.2 per cent between now and the year 2001. However, the increase in some age groups is much greater than this. The number of people aged between 85 and 89 is expected to increase by nearly 12 per cent and the number of people aged 90 or over is expected to increase by 65 per cent. This will greatly increase the demand for nursing and residential care for the elderly, a field in which many small businesses are well established. You should contact your local authority social services department to acquaint yourself with the needs and opportunities in this area.

Matching agencies

These are organisations which bring together people who have ideas on the one hand and those who have resources such as money and experience on the other. Some of the propositions are high risk/high reward. Others are simply too small to attract equity funding from institutions but represent an opportunity for a redundant person with experience and money to invest in the business. The responsibility lies firmly with the potential investor to evaluate the proposal, though in most cases the organisations who are active in this field, notably *Venture Capital Report* and *The Enterprise Agency Marriage Bureaux*, provide a lot of background information and advice to help you make your decision. See Chapter 3 for further details.

Self-employment in selling

A person with experience in selling can seek opportunities for self-employment, possibly in the field which he or she has left or a related one, using the *British Agents Register* or the *Manufacturers' Agents Association* to find suitable organisations to represent. These openings are usually found in markets where most manufacturers/suppliers are small and cannot afford their own sales force; and/or where the retailers or other distributors are fragmented and it is economic to have one representative carrying the lines of several companies. This can also apply with imported goods. Chinaware, giftware, books and household textiles are examples. See Chapter 3 for further information.

Franchising

Under a franchise agreement a *franchisee* buys the right to use a business system which has been tried and tested by someone else, the *franchisor*. Franchise operations are commonly established in fields where personal commitment of the kind expected of a small business is recognised as essential to success. Catering and service industries are particularly well represented in the franchise sector. There is a wide variety from which to choose, and many excellent guides to the subject are available. For further information see Chapter 3.

The idea sellers

Several organisations exist which offer to sell more or less 'off-the-peg' ideas to start your own business. The one thing that most of them have in common is a tendency to make lavish promises of wealth and success if you will only buy their ideas. The quality varies greatly. The only safe advice is:

1. Beware of anyone who makes extravagant claims in advertisements. Enthusiasm is to be expected but anyone who offers to make you 'master of your own destiny' or promises to tell you how to make a lot of money in a short time with very little work is to be treated with great caution.
2. Before parting with any money, try to see a sample of what is on offer. If the supplier is confident of the value of what he is offering he won't mind showing it to you. If he won't do this you are wise to hold on to your money.

3. Subscriptions or books sold by mail order through newspaper advertisements nearly always have a 'money back if not satisfied' provision in them at the insistence of the newspapers in which they appear. If you order through a newspaper, make a note of the address to which you send your payment (the address is not always printed in the book you are sent) and request a refund if you are disappointed with what you receive. Chapter 5 contains information on some of these organisations in Britain, France and the USA. If you are seriously considering a certain kind of enterprise (for example, a florist's or a sandwich bar) and you find that one of the idea sellers commended in Chapter 5 has reported on it, then the information may prove to be of value, even if it comes from France or the USA. However, you should always carry out independent research of your own as well since market factors are constantly changing.

Licensing opportunities

A number of organisations in Britain, France and the USA publicise products or ideas on behalf of manufacturers who are unable to market them themselves. For example, a company in the United States may develop a product which it is in no position to market in the UK. Alternatively, a very large company may, in the course of its research, throw up an idea which is too small to be of value to the company itself. In this case, the company will frequently offer the idea to a small organisation under a licensing arrangement. Most of these are technical products which would be best suited for adoption by a small company aiming to diversify. However, some of them would be suitable as start-up opportunities for people with suitable experience. These are examined in Chapter 4.

Creative ways of looking at ideas

Now that you have started thinking of ideas, look at each concept from many different points of view. Here is a list of variables to consider when thinking about a product or service. This list does not include every approach and you will certainly think of additional questions. Write them down so you can refer back to them. Ask yourself the following questions:

How can I . . .

*   make it safer, cleaner, slower or faster?
*   make it at home and save overhead expense?
*   contract other people to make the product or perform the service at their home?
*   teach it more quickly?

- make it more convenient or inexpensive?
- make it more pleasant?
- cut costs of material and labour?
- combine it with or add it on to other products or services?
- make it automatic?
- make it easier to package, store, transport?
- make it self-contained, portable, mobile or disposable?
- condense or enlarge its size?
- make it easier to use?
- make it less expensive to replace, repair or reuse?
- make it easier to clean, maintain, lubricate or adjust?
- make it more attractive and appealing?
- make it lighter, stronger, adjustable, thinner or foldable?
- make it quieter or louder?
- minimise its potential hazards?
- exert less effort, time, and energy when dealing with it?
- add new features?
- make it reversible?
- make it dual or multi-functional?
- sell it more cheaply for more benefit (eg two for the price of one)?
- remove any irritating feature or side-effects?
- improve its availability or distribution?
- improve its production?
- improve its design?
- improve its marketing?
- improve it in other ways?

The above checklist is reprinted from *The Entrepreneur's Complete Self-Assessment Guide* by Douglas A Gray (Kogan Page) 1987.

Personal qualities of the entrepreneur

Having established that there are many opportunities available for small businesses which will be examined in greater detail in the chapters which follow, you still have to decide whether you have the personal qualities required to make a success of it. The case studies in Chapter 10 convey the features of self-employment as experienced by some people who are comparatively new to it. There are four main issues which you must consider, each with a positive and negative side.

Independence and insecurity

The desire to 'be my own boss' is a strong reason for starting a business. You take your own decisions and do not have to explain or justify them to bosses or committees unless you make so many bad decisions that your bank manager starts to become difficult. You do not have to attend meetings or write reports, the twin curses of middle management. Now that I run my own business I look back with humour but without regret to the time when my working life was dominated by these necessary but tedious activities.

On the other hand, there is no one to blame when things go wrong and no one with whom to share the responsibility. If the business fails, you lose not only your income, but any assets (eg your house) you have offered as security. You receive no redundancy payment and you may not even qualify for unemployment benefit. Much of this book is devoted to ways of minimising the chances of failure but if you value security far above independence, self-employment is probably wrong for you.

Hard work and high rewards

Paul Getty is credited with the claim that the only way to become really rich is to work for yourself. It is true that very successful entrepreneurs do become far wealthier than they would by remaining as employees, but they do so at the cost of very hard work. Those who simply earn a modest living from self-employment also work long hours as can be seen from the case studies in Chapter 10. On the other hand, I know from my own experience that work does not seem quite so hard when you are doing it for yourself, knowing that any rewards will benefit you rather than someone else. Nevertheless, if regular hours of work are important elements in your life, you should avoid self-employment.

Broad responsibilities and limited experience

Small businesses, like large ones, need a wide variety of skills and experience – production, marketing, record keeping, finance and ac-counting, personnel etc. In large companies each is discharged by an expert in that field. In a small company, it is likely that the owner will be deeply involved in all of them. This can be exhilarating. It can also be dangerous if he believes that his natural talent and personal charm are adequate substitutes for knowledge.

The owner who recognises his shortcomings is not a problem since he can devise a strategy which will fill the gap in his knowledge. He can do this by employing experts like accountants or advertising agents; or by taking into partnership someone with complementary skills; or, as in my own case, by marrying the right person!

The small businessman who does not recognise that he has imperfections and trusts only himself to carry out all the tasks is the one who runs into trouble. However, I suspect that such people do not in any case listen to advice or read books like this one so I doubt if you fall into this category! To avoid their fate, I recommend that you ask yourself two questions:

1.   In which of the major business areas listed below do you have most experience, little experience or no experience?

- Production of the goods or services you plan to market (or retailing experience if this is the field you choose).
- Selling and other forms of customer contact.
- Advertising, public relations and other forms of communication.
- Bookkeeping.
- Financial planning.
- Administration.
- Technical aspects (if applicable).
- Personnel management, including recruitment.

2.   What steps will you take to fill these gaps?

- Self-development, eg courses – but you can't do everything.
- Using outside help.
- Going into partnership with someone who has complementary skills.
- Employing someone with complementary skills.

Determination and tunnel vision
Determination in the face of adversity is an important asset in founding a business. Yet this admirable quality is closely related to an obsessive belief in one's own judgement and a contempt for that of others. People with this quality discover new continents and invent the wheel, but they can also be impossible to work with and they often go bankrupt as a result of ignoring wise advice. Every small business centre is familiar with them. Some of them are mad inventors who are angry with the world for not recognising their genius. Others are convinced that they can outshine Marks and Spencer through inspiration or force of personality.

Some of the organisations described in Chapter 9, such as enterprise agencies and the Small Firms Service, exist to prevent such dreams from turning into nightmares. If, after reading this chapter, you are attracted by the prospect of starting your own business and believe that you will avoid the negative factors mentioned above, then the remainder of this book is designed to help you.

Chapter 2

Markets Suited to Small Businesses

What are the factors which signify that a certain type of activity is suited to a small firm? Since this book is mainly concerned with firms that are just starting up or are in an early phase of expansion, a ceiling of ten employees has been taken as a working figure for manufacturing businesses.

If we accept this definition as a working arrangement, then small firms are clearly excluded from some activities demanding large-scale production – steel and oil, for example. Yet, other activities which appear to be suited to small firms are in fact perilous. An example of this is the village shop or corner shop briefly referred to on page 8.

Independent food retailers are penalised merely for being small. They pay their suppliers much higher prices than the multiple retailers. The buying power of multiples is used, perfectly legally, to intimidate suppliers into granting them more favourable terms than are justified by any economies suppliers can make in selling to them. The result is lower prices for the consumer, accompanied by the closure of many small shops. There is no reason to expect that there will be any significant change in this trend in the future. Some independents have survived and prospered by turning themselves into neighbourhood or convenience stores, opening long hours and offering newspapers and videos.

However, unless one of these expedients is adopted, the future of the independent grocer's shop is far from secure even though, superficially, it is a suitable outlet for the energies of the would-be entrepreneur. There are increasing signs that the retailing of other goods, such as electrical products and mass market clothing, are going the same way.

This book seeks to identify those activities which appear to offer a reasonable prospect of success to a small, possibly new, enterprise. Government data were examined to identify those market sectors where:

- at present, small firms account for an above average share of employment or output;
- there is evidence that the market share held by small firms is stable

or increasing and/or that the overall market is itself growing, thus offering more opportunities for new enterprises;

• there are any common factors which make certain activities particularly appropriate for *small* businesses.

The analysis is divided into the following sections:

1.　A survey of growth areas, followed by an analysis of:
2.　Manufacturing
3.　Retailing
4.　Catering
5.　Other services (a very important sector for small firms as we have seen).

This analysis has involved the examination of more volumes of government statistics than most people will ever need to see.

Some conclusions have been drawn about the patterns of small business activity which emerge from the figures. The figures themselves are shown in the tables to which the reader may turn for further information, following the reference in the text. Finally, the really stout-hearted can use the references in the tables to find the original government publication for further information.

Publications are referred to throughout by the reference codes used by HMSO, the government bookshop. For example, PA 1003 is an annual survey of UK businesses broken down by size of the workforce. SDA 25 is the enquiry into retailing.

A survey of growth areas

By examining the government publication PA 1003, *Size Analysis of UK Businesses*, April 1989, it is possible to establish those industrial sectors in which the number of businesses has significantly increased. This is based on the VAT register and thus includes all but the very smallest enterprises. The relevant figures are shown in Table 2.1 on page 25.

It is immediately apparent that, whereas there has been an increase in the number of enterprises in all these categories over the period concerned, the increase has been particularly striking, both in absolute numbers and in percentage terms, in the service sector. These figures will be examined more closely later. There has also been substantial growth in construction, though this is no doubt a reflection of the property boom which occurred during the 1980s and, as the property market became depressed in 1988–89, one would expect the number of construction companies to flatten out or decline.

Having examined the growth in businesses further light can be cast on the sectors concerned by looking at the trend in the total number of jobs. The figures in Table 2.2 are taken from the *Annual Abstract of Statistics*, 1989,

Table 2.1

Category	Number of VAT registered units 1980	Number of VAT units 1988	Percentage change
Manufacturing	144,038	161,534	+12
Construction	199,036	238,052	+20
Road transport and transport services	59,555	68,165	+14
Wholesaling and dealing	103,258	129,335	+25
Finance, property and professional services	89,412	133,283	+49
Catering	118,673	128,202	+ 8
Other services	138,161	222,647	+61

Source: *Size Analysis of UK Businesses*, April 1989

Table 6.2, and show the sectors in which employment (the total number of jobs) grew by 10 per cent or more in the period 1982–87 – a slightly shorter period than that referred to in the previous section but broadly comparable with it. It is worth bearing in mind that, during this five year period, total employment in all industries and services increased by less than 2 per cent while it actually declined by 14 per cent in production industries. Any sector which managed to generate 10 per cent more jobs may therefore be defined as a prosperous and promising one.

Table 2.2

Category	No of jobs 1982	No of jobs 1987	Percentage increase
Restaurant, cafes, snack bars	194,000	238,000	+23
Pubs and bars	236,000	282,000	+19
Hotels	229,000	261,000	+14
Repair of consumer goods and vehicles	205,000	245,000	+20
Banking and finance	467,000	548,000	+17
Professional business services	588,000	772,000	+31
Other business services	301,000	500,000	+66

Source: *Annual Abstract of Statistics*, 1989, Table 6.2

In a period in which employment in all industries and services increased by less than 2 per cent there were a number of sectors which experienced phenomenal growth and it is to these that we must look for the businesses and jobs of the future. Moreover, many of those identified are in sectors in which small firms do well. This is evident from the New Earnings Survey 1988, described in the *Employment Gazette* in January 1989. This showed that, whereas organisations employing fewer than ten people accounted for 6.5 per cent of all the enterprises in the survey, they accounted for nearly 14 per cent of those employed in the fields of distribution, hotels, catering and repairs. This is where much of the growth is occurring.

Manufacturing

Having surveyed the data overall, let us now look at individual sectors, starting with manufacturing. Most production industries have seen a decline in employment in the 1980s as productivity has improved and as Britain's manufacturing base has shrunk. Small increases have been registered in the timber and wooden furniture industries which have seen an increase of 3.5 per cent and in the rubber and plastics sector which has seen growth of 9.5 per cent (*Annual Abstract of Statistics*, 1989, Table 6.2).

What is more interesting, however, is to isolate those manufacturing sectors in which small firms, with fewer than ten employees, account for an above average proportion of jobs. Within the manufacturing sector as a whole during 1988, units (that is to say workshops, factories etc) with fewer than ten employees accounted for 6.8 per cent of total employment. In Table 2.3 are listed those sectors in which these small units, with fewer than ten workers, accounted for at least 10 per cent of jobs – significantly higher than the average for manufacturing as a whole. The list can be used to identify those manufacturing sectors in which, on first appraisal, small firms are well established and in which, therefore, smallness is presumably not a disadvantage. A number of entries which show interesting and perhaps surprising results include:

Agricultural machinery: 19 per cent of jobs are in units of fewer than ten workers.

Metal working machine tools: 20 per cent of jobs are in units of under ten workers. (This is possibly a reflection of the high degree of skill required in producing certain machine tools.)

Bread and flour confectionery: 12 per cent of jobs in units of under ten workers.

Ice-cream: 18 per cent of jobs in units of fewer than ten workers. (The last two entries possibly reflect recent trends towards market segmentation in these fields and the consolidation of some large companies' activities in these markets.)

Manufacture of leather goods excluding footwear: 21 per cent of jobs in units of less than ten workers. (Again an operation which depends upon skilled workers.)

Builders' carpentry and joinery: 15 per cent of jobs in units of under ten
workers. (A large proportion of the timber trades are characterised by
small units: no doubt this is a reflection of the skill involved in producing
custom-made units for clients.)

Printing and publishing of books: 13 per cent of jobs in units of under ten
workers.

In addition, the obviously *craft*-orientated categories such as jewellery and
musical instrument making have many of their jobs in small units as do
virtually all the miscellaneous categories – minerals, metals, engineering,
textiles, dress etc.

The full list is as follows. In each case the Standard Industrial Classification
(SIC) Number is quoted so that the reader can follow up the entry in
government publications if required.

Table 2.3

SIC	Description	Units with 1–9 employees (*Account for the number and proportion of jobs stated below*)
3138	Heat and surface treatment of metals, inc sintering	2,015 = 11.2%
3169	Miscellaneous finished metal products	15,424 = 17%
3205	Boilers and processed plant fabrication	4,728 = 10.1%
3211	Agricultural machinery	1,687 = 18.9%
3221	Metalworking machine tools	5,058 = 19.7%
3222	Engineers' small tools	3,634 = 10.9%
3261	Precision chains and other mechanical power transmission equipment	6,862 = 20.8%
3289	Miscellaneous mechanical, marine and precision equipment	15,248 = 24.7%
3470/80	Electric lamps and installation equipment	3,289 = 11.7%
4121	Slaughterhouses	1,765 = 11.1%
4196	Bread and flour confectionery	13,394 = 12.2%
4213	Ice-cream	647 = 18.2%
4399	Miscellaneous textiles	1,518 = 24.3%
4420	Leather goods	2,354 = 20.9%
4533	Women's and girls' tailored outerwear	3,677 = 14.9%
4536	Women's and girls' light outerwear, lingerie and infants' wear	10,805 = 13.2%

SIC	Description	Units with 1–9 employees (*Account for the number and proportion of jobs stated below*)
4539	Other dress industries	2,584 = 13.1%
4556	Canvas sacks, goods and made-up textiles	1,452 = 21.4%
4610	Milling and planing wood	3,391 = 14.9%
4620	Wood processing and treatment	527 = 11.1%
4630	Builders' carpentry and joinery	4,862 = 14.9%
4640	Wooden containers	2,816 = 16.8%
4650	Other wooden articles excluding furniture	3,224 = 31.6%
4671	Wooden and upholstered furniture	12,585 = 14.8%
4672	Shop and office fittings	2,539 = 10.8%
4752	Printing and publishing periodicals	4,330 = 11.3%
4753	Printing and publishing books	4,893 = 13.3%
4910	Jewellery and coins	4,711 = 32.9%
4920	Musical instrument manufacture	578 = 22.2%
4930	Photoprocessing labs	1,420 = 10.1%
4941	Manufacture of toys and games	1,086 = 10.3%

Summary

It is difficult to see an overall pattern amid such a diverse range of activity but the following factors are common to more than one of the sectors mentioned:

1. Products and markets too small to interest big companies: for example, many *miscellaneous* categories.
2. Products in which small market segments are, or are becoming, important and/or in which local distribution is important, for example, ice-cream and bread/flour confectionery. Some big companies have ceased or reduced their activities in these markets in recent years, leaving behind pockets of opportunity for small firms. This trend has been further promoted by increasing preferences among consumers for fresh products which are unadulterated by additives and preservatives. This puts a premium on flexible operation and quick deliveries over restricted areas which are more easily handled by small local organisations than by large manufacturers with large capital intensive plants remote from the area of consumption. Another example, from a different market, is

that of film processing. This service requires equipment which can be fitted into a small high street unit and the rapid service offered by local units of this kind can outweigh the economies of scale resulting from a massive centralised operation.

3. Products in which *custom-made* or *one-off* products may be needed on a small scale and where the flexibility of a small firm outweighs the larger firm's economies of scale: for example, shopfitters. Most shops are still independently owned and to that extent resistant to systems retailing. For further analysis see the section on retailing which follows.

4. Products in which changes in taste and/or fashion require flexibility and design input rather than mass output, eg women's clothing.

5. Sectors in which a high degree of skill is required on the part of the individual operator and which do not lend themselves to capital-intensive mechanisation. Examples of this are high quality clothing and leather goods.

Table 2.4
The following analysis, based on data from the 1989 *Annual Abstract of Statistics* and on SDA 25 *Retailing Enquiry*, Table 3, lists those retail sectors where the average number of outlets per business is less than 1.5 – in other words where single outlet retailers predominate.

Retail sector	Outlets per business	Examples of the category
Dairymen	1.1	Express Dairy
Butchers, poulterers	1.3	Dewhursts
Fishmongers	1.2	
Greengrocers, fruiterers	1.2	Gerrards
Bread and flour confectioners	1.3	Millers Hot Bread Kitchen
Confectioners, tobacconists, newsagents (CTNs)	1.2	NSS, Martins
Leather and travel goods	1.3	Salisbury Handbags
Carpets	1.2	Queensway
Furniture	1.3	Habitat, Courts, MFI
Hardware/china/fancy goods	1.2	Robert Dyas, British Gas
DIY	1.4	Homebase, B & Q
Newagents/stationers	1.3	Rymans
Booksellers	1.2	Heffers
Toys, hobbies, sports and cycles	1.2	Toys R Us
Florists, seeds, nurseries	1.2	Cramphorns

The examples are given to illustrate what some of the categories mean since this is not always self-evident. However, they also help to show that in some sectors where one is very conscious of multiples, like women's clothing, small businesses remain very important in some parts of the market.

Retailing

Retailing has been one of the most prosperous sectors of the economy in the 1980s and some of the best known high street names have been among the Stock Exchange's favourites. Nevertheless, it is an area in which to tread with care. As previously observed, the retailing of groceries, electrical goods and mass market clothing are sectors which the small independent enters at his peril. The analysis in the pages which follow is based on the government's publication SDA 25 *Retailing Enquiry* published in 1989. I have attempted to identify those retail sectors where one or more of the following conditions applies:

1.   Where the sector is dominated by independent traders.
2.   Where the number of outlets is increasing in number – an indication of prosperity.
3.   Sectors in which single outlet retailers enjoy a market share above the average of 28.5 per cent held by single outlet retailers overall.

These facts are set out in Tables 2.4 to 2.6 and I have followed them with some general conclusions.

Table 2.5   *Sectors in which the number of outlets or jobs is increasing*
SDA 25 *Retailing Enquiry* (1989) gives the latest information available for the retail trade. It reveals that in 1986 there were 244,006 retail businesses with 343,387 outlets employing 2,334,000 people. This was a drop from 1980 of 12,133 outlets and 74,000 jobs, and continues a long-term trend. In 1961 2,767,000 people worked in retailing. However, within these totals there were some sectors in which the number of outlets/jobs either remained stable or increased. These were:

Category	Outlets		Jobs	
	1980	**1986**	**1980**	**1986**
Fishmongers, poulterers	2,866	3,158	8,000	8,000
CTNs	48,351	47,774	220,000	234,000
Off-licences	8,024	8,736	29,000	34,000
General clothing businesses	7,767	11,282	50,000	73,000
Footwear	11,908	11,447	76,000	80,000
Leather and travel goods	1,748	1,753	5,000	5,000
Carpets	4,792	5,152	22,000	21,000
Electrical, gas and music goods	15,928	16,304	77,000	89,000
Chemists	11,694	12,538	67,000	77,000
Booksellers, stationers, newsagents	6,325	7,483	35,000	37,000
Jewellers	7,746	8,096	41,000	38,000
Hire or repair (exc TV hire)	1,447	1,813	6,000	6,000

Table 2.6   *Market share*
Single outlet retailers account for 28.5 per cent of total retail business. The following table shows the market share broken down by trade sector. From this, it is possible to identify those retail sectors in which single outlet retailers performed significantly better than average. On the face of it, therefore, this is an indication that it is a sector which is more suited than most to the small retailer.

Commodity or service sold	Percentage market share of single outlet retailer
Total retail turnover	28.5
Fresh fruit and vegetables	33.7
Fresh milk and cream	40.8
Fresh meat, poultry and game	35
Fresh fish	49.5
Chocolate and sugar confectionery	46.2
Tobacco and smokers' requisites	41.4
Newspapers and periodicals	61.7
Drugs, medicines, toilet preparations etc	46.5
Carpets, carpeting and rugs	44.2
Household textiles and soft furnishings	30.8
Hardware, china, glassware and cutlery	36
Cut flowers, plants, seeds and garden sundries	54.8
Antiques, works of arts, stamps and coins	83.4
Novelties, souvenirs, gifts etc	43.2
Books	37.7
Stationery and office supplies	36.6
Jewellery, silverware, watches and clocks	41.8
Sports goods, toys, games, cycles and camping equipment	42.2

The following factors appear to be significant in contributing to the success of independent retailers:

- *Hours of work.* Long, unsocial hours are characteristic of many independent-dominated sectors: CTNs, dairies, butchers, poulterers, fishmongers, florists, seedsmen and nurseries (in which weekends, including Sundays, are important). The need for overtime payments makes these long hours unattractive to multiple traders; there is little reason to expect change here given the failure of the Sunday Trading Bill so it appears that an ability to wake up early and work long hours will continue to be an important ingredient in succeeding as an independent retailer.
- *Resale price maintenance.* This effectively protects booksellers and newsagents from price-cutting competition by multiples and thereby confers an advantage on independent retailers in these

sectors compared with those in other markets such as food retailing.

- *Product differentiation.* Where purchases are occasional and prices less critical than choice, it appears that the independent retailer can have an advantage: gifts, china, glassware and jewellery are examples, though the success of Ratners in capturing an ever-increasing share of the jewellery market by price cutting leaves some doubt whether this will continue to be a good sector for the independent except in upmarket, specialised sectors. Another area which is doing very well is that of card retailing where a number of small organisations have carved out profitable niches for themselves, made possible by the very high gross profits available in this sector.
- *Specialist knowledge or service.* Cycles, lawnmowers, antiques, books, sports, camping, plants.
- *After-sales service.* Household textiles and soft furnishings, garden products, cycles, carpets, hire and repair businesses (eg hire of DIY equipment).

It is worth remarking that independents are surprisingly well established in some sectors which are traditionally thought to be dominated by multiples. For example, in the market for women's, girls', children's and infants' wear, single outlet retailers command a market share of 24 per cent – only slightly below the average despite the fact that large chains like Marks and Spencer, Next, Principles etc, appear to dominate. The reason is that independents are still very strongly established in the fashion and designer sectors where choice, taste and service predominate.

Catering

Table 2.7 contains information on catering and related trades taken from the 1989 *Annual Abstract of Statistics*. Published government statistics on the catering trades are not as extensive as those on manufacturing or retailing. In particular, it is not possible to isolate, from published data, the performance of small or single outlet caterers as distinct from the large chains. Nevertheless, one's own observations make it possible to deduce those sectors in which small organisations are well represented or predominant. The figures are given below and show the growth in the number of businesses and in their turnover from 1980 to 1986 both for the catering trade as a whole and for its components.

The figures show that, while the industry as a whole is doing very well, the greatest growth area was undoubtedly in the *take-away sector*. The number of businesses increased by 25 per cent and the turnover by 120 per cent, far outperforming any other catering sector. Moreover, this is the sector which

Table 2.7

Trade	No of Businesses			Turnover (£m)		
	1980	1986	% change	1980	1986	% change
Total	109,471	119,889	9.5	£12,424	£20,971	+68.7
Hotels and other residential establishments	14,281	12,855	−10	£ 2,483	£ 4,279	+72
Holiday camps, camping and caravan sites	1,587	1,621	+ 2.1	£ 405	£ 567	+40
Restaurants, cafes etc for food consumption on premises	11,512	14,348	+24.6	£ 1,431	£ 2,260	+57.9
Take-aways inc fish and chips and sandwich bars	22,715	28,436	+25.1	£ 1,103	£ 2,435	+120
Pubs	40,608	42,901	+ 5.6	£ 4,857	£ 8,043	+65.5
Clubs	17,571	18,002	+ 2.4	£ 1,570	£ 2,203	+40.3
Catering contractors	1,196	1,727	+44.3	£ 575	£ 1,183	+106

one's own observations show to be dominated by independent, family-run businesses such as the multitude of sandwich bars which have sprung up in cities to serve office workers and tourists; and also by franchised outlets such as Wimpy, Perfect Pizza etc. Since franchise businesses, described in more detail in Chapter 3, offer a form of independence, this further confirms the success of independent businesses in this booming area of our economy.

If you have any interest in the hotel and catering industry, the Industry Training Board (HCITB) produces a series of valuable surveys of the industry which should be read by anyone thinking of entering this sector. Among other things, their publications identify those parts of the country which are over – and under – provided with the services. The HCITB can be contacted at International House, High Street, Ealing, London W5 5DB; 081–672 4251.

Other service industries

As we have seen, the service sector is one of the most rapidly growing in the British economy and offers many opportunities for new small enterprises. It is also a notoriously difficult one to analyse in detail from published statistics. There are two reasons for this. First, the sector covers an exceptionally diverse range of activities from architects and advertising agencies to photographers and undertakers. Second, published government statistics are in very broad categories which make it very difficult or impossible to identify individual business sectors. However, by careful use of the information which is available, it is possible to isolate some sectors which are rapidly growing in sufficient detail to indicate the existence of a potential market for new small enterprises.

The first such sector is defined as *professional business services*. Employment in this group increased by 31 per cent in the period 1982–87 (compared with less than 2 per cent for the economy as a whole) so it can clearly be seen that this is a sector which is in a growth phase. Businesses in this category include estate agents (a somewhat volatile occupation); surveyors and valuers; lawyers, architects, accountants and bookkeepers.

A second category which is growing even more rapidly is defined as *other business services*. Employment in this group increased by *66 per cent* in the same five-year period. This category includes advertising agencies; computer services and bureaux; copy and duplicating services; market research; management consultancy; translation and typing services. These enterprises are all in the so-called 'tertiary' sector of the economy, selling skills to our longer established businesses in more mature manufacturing and retailing sectors. A survey of enterprise agencies described in Chapter 9 confirms that a large number of new enterprises are continuing to be set up in these two sectors.

A 23 per cent growth in employment in 1982–87 was apparent in the sector described in official statistics as *renting of movables*. This can involve hiring anything from cameras, television and power tools to tractors and combine harvesters. Although some of these are beyond the scale of the small business, it is evident that many towns now have hire shops which loan out specialised, DIY gardening and decorating equipment to householders and this is a sector which seems to be expanding.

Finally, the sector described as *personal services* saw a growth in employment of nearly 10 per cent. Besides some well-established business sectors such as laundries, dry-cleaners and hairdressers in which employment is believed to be reasonably static, this sector includes others where the growth presumably lies: photographic enterprises; boarding kennels; beauty parlours; entertainment.

This analysis is supported by a detailed study of VAT records which was carried out by the former statistician of the Small Firms Service, Mr Pom Ganguly, and was published in *British Business* on 5 July 1985. This showed that the most rapid growth in the number of businesses was occurring in advertising and market research (+44 per cent); duplicating, calculating and typewriting services (+36 per cent); computer services (+255 per cent); management consultants (+52 per cent); and entertainment (+58 per cent).

Summary
The purpose of this chapter has been to draw attention to those activities in which small firms are well established and in which there appears to be room for further growth. It has shown that opportunities exist in many markets, particularly in the catering and services sectors.

CHAPTER 3

Matching Ideas and Resources

There are many ways in which people with resources such as money, experience or contacts can be matched with those who have need of them. This is, in effect, a way of starting a business by teaming up with others who need what you have to offer. Three of these methods are examined here: matching organisations, selling agencies and franchises.

Matching organisations

A number of organisations specialise in matching business partners. People with ideas which they wish to develop or existing businesses they wish to expand are put in touch with others who have appropriate money or skills available. Two of these are described below.

Venture Capital Report (VCR)

VCR is published from Henley-on-Thames by Venture Capital Report Ltd. It was started in 1978 by its present director, Lucius Cary, who has an MBA from Harvard Business School and worked for Hanson Trust before starting up a small chain of restaurants. The difficulty he experienced in raising finance for his restaurants led him to start VCR.

VCR is published each month and sent to subscribers who pay £200 a year if they are resident in the UK, £220 in Europe and £240 elsewhere. Estimated readership is 5000. It is advertised in the Financial Times, Sunday Times, Executive Post and by direct mail.

Each issue of VCR contains a detailed analysis of about seven or eight businesses seeking investment funds and, often, seeking management expertise from the investor. These write-ups are prepared by Lucius Cary or one of his five regional agents, who bear comparable qualifications, and they are the product of interviews and meetings covering many hours. They describe the company's history (where it is already trading): the background and experience of its principals; its products; its present position; its investment needs and its projections. The analyses are very professionally done, pointing out risks as well as opportunities. A good deal of financial information is included together with illustrations and technical descriptions of products where required. The work is very time-consuming and demands highly skilled and experienced people to do it.

A small charge is made to the entrepreneur seeking funds to cover the costs of the write-ups – £100 for start-ups and £200 for business expansions. Those who succeed in attracting funds from subscribers to the magazine pay a commission proportionate to the investment. During the course of a full year, about 2000 initial enquiries are received from people who seek investment funds but by the time these have been examined by Mr Cary and his associates, only about 100 will receive write-ups in *VCR*. The July 1989 issue contained seven case histories including the following:

- *Green directories.* The publisher of a directory of green products and services which was published in Hamburg, Germany in 1987 now wants to launch some of the regional directories in the UK. £30,000 is sought in return for 30 per cent of the equity, 1 per cent of the equity for every £1000 invested.
- *Refuse compactors.* A company selling refuse compactors seeks £25,000 to finance stocks and to increase marketing of its own compactor design. 25 per cent of the equity is offered.
- *Computer system sales.* An ex-teacher with five years' computing experience started a company in April 1989 to sell computer systems to schools and dentists. He seeks £95,000 to finance expansion of the business and £150,000 to move to new premises. 40 per cent of the equity is offered.
- *Children's cars.* A company producing high-class electrically powered children's cars requires £80,000–£200,000 working capital to finance incoming orders and to increase marketing of the products. About 25 per cent of the equity is offered in return for the investment.

In addition, each issue of *VCR* contains a mid-page article on a subject of interest to venture capital investors. Contributors include Matthew Symonds, Deputy Editor of the *Independent*; Sir Leon Brittan, Vice-President of the European Commission; and Professor Heinz Wolff of Brunel Institute of Bio-engineering.

Companies using *VCR* are likely to have had difficulty raising investment from other sources such as banks or stockbrokers. This is sometimes because their needs are too small. Banks and stockbrokers are not really interested in investments (as distinct from loans) of much less than £100,000. Alternatively, applicants may use *VCR* because the projects are high risk or lack tangible assets as security. The risks may be high, but so can be the rewards. Subscribers to *VCR* may at least be reassured by the realism and professionalism of the analyses and write-ups which provide the essential ingredients in the operation. *VCR* has a licence to operate from the Department of Trade and Industry, which is a legal requirement since it is effectively inviting people to invest in businesses.

Venture Capital Report can be seen in the Science Reference Library, 25 Southampton Buildings, Chancery Lane, London WC2A 1AW. Subscription enquiries should be directed to Venture Capital Report who are located at Boston Road, Henley-on-Thames, Oxfordshire RG9 1DY; 0491 579999.

LINC – Local Investment Networking Company

Enterprise agencies, whose activities are described in more detail in Chapter 9, aim to promote business and jobs. Sixteen of them have got together to run the LINC organisation, a nationwide business introduction service which aims to help small businesses find capital and management help. It is aimed specifically at businesses who are seeking equity investments up to £150,000. The scheme operates as follows:

Entrepreneurs who seek finance are invited to produce a business plan showing clearly the amount of funds required together with the history of the business, the people who run it and the products or services offered. Enterprise agencies who belong to the LINC organisation give guidance to entrepreneurs on drawing up the plan. Such advice is free of charge. A monthly bulletin is issued which briefly describes each proposal. The July 1989 bulletin contained 93 such proposals of which the following are a few examples:

- £40,000 to launch a new company in organic fertilisers
- £150,000 required for a new company producing toys and games
- £70,000 to expand a small trade and technical publisher serving a specialised market
- £75,000 to expand a successful mail order company
- £50,000 to expand a manufacturer of printed circuit boards
- £150,000 to open a fast food restaurant in London.

The entrepreneurs who are trying to raise capital in this way are required to pay a one-off registration fee of £50. In addition to the 60-word description of the business which is placed on a marketing bulletin, the small business is also required to produce a two-page business summary which is retained by LINC and sent on request to all registered potential investors. If an investor is interested in the proposal, he will then contact the small business direct.

Potential investors who wish to receive the bulletin are required to have between £10,000 and £150,000 available to invest. Many of the subscribers are referred by accountants, banks and headhunters, the last sometimes referring redundant executives who have golden handshakes to invest.

Investors pay a registration fee of £50 per annum to receive the bulletin. In addition to the bulletin, the enterprise agencies who are part of the network sometimes invite entrepreneurs to make presentations to potential investors. Each entrepreneur is given 20–30 minutes to present his or her case and to answer questions. At one such meeting attended by the author at the London Enterprise Agency, six presentations were made including a long-established retail jeweller; a greetings card company; a life assurance broker; a publisher; and a mail order magazine.

The London Enterprise Agency (LENTA) was in fact one of the first agencies to introduce this concept of matching entrepreneurs and potential investors. In its early days, it was known as the LENTA Marriage Bureau and this term is still in use. Other enterprise agencies developed similar ideas and eventually they came together to form the LINC network. The agencies currently involved in the network are listed below. Their full addresses and telephone numbers are given in Chapter 9.

Aberdeen Enterprise Trust
Bolton Business Ventures Ltd
Cardiff and Vale Enterprise
Cleveland Enterprise Agency
Dudley Business Venture
Glasgow Opportunities
London Enterprise Agency (LENTA)
Manchester Business Venture
Medway Enterprise Agency Ltd
Merseyside Education Training Enterprise Ltd
Northamptonshire Enterprise Agency Ltd
Sheffield Enterprise Agency (SENTA)
South Somerset and West Dorset Enterprise Agency
West Cornwall Enterprise Trust Ltd

In addition, these agencies operate a data base which endeavours to match each investment opportunity with the most suitable investor.

Summary
These two organisations, VCR and LINC, bring together those who have business ideas and those who have money and expertise. A wide variety of opportunities is covered both in type and size of business. VCR provides a very professional analysis of the businesses concerned. Like VCR the LINC organisation has no financial interest in the organisations whose needs its publicises, though the descriptions of the businesses in the LINC bulletin are more dependent upon the assessment of the entrepreneur himself than those of VCR whose staff carry out extensive investigations into the companies. Nevertheless, both organisations emphasise that the

responsibility for making the final judgement rests firmly with the investor who must contact the business himself.

These organisations could be used by a person such as a redundant manager with several years' specialised experience in a skill needed by a small company, with funds to invest (perhaps redundancy money) and with the ability to evaluate risk.

Establishing a selling agency

The Manufacturers' Agents Association (MAA)

The MAA was established in 1909 for the benefit of bona fide manufacturers' agents – self-employed agents who sell the products of one or more manufacturers, usually in return for commission. It advises its members on drawing up contracts with their principals, how to advertise their services and other matters concerned with their interests. The annual subscription is £34.50 with a £28.75 joining fee.

The MAA also publishes a monthly magazine called *The Manufacturers' Agent* which contains advertisements by companies seeking agents to represent them in various areas and markets. The June 1989 issue contained about 16 such advertisements for a variety of manufacturers including:

- A company seeking agents to sell radiators to builders' merchants.
- Agents in all areas of the UK to promote non-allergenic herbal toiletries to retailers.
- A company requiring agents to sell laboratory products to manufacturing, academic, medical and other outlets.
- Belgian, French, Danish and Israeli companies seeking agents to sell their products in the UK.

Many business sectors, especially those containing a large number of small producers such as textiles, giftware, furniture and books, depend heavily upon self-employed agents for their sales. People made redundant with some years of selling experience can consider setting themselves up as agents either in the field in which they previously worked or in one related to it. For example, a man with previous experience of selling haberdashery could also sell fabrics to his trade contacts. A person who has sold cards and stationery items could sell giftware to the same outlets. Businesses with fragmented manufacturing or distribution channels are likely to make use of agents. These may be recognised by a reference to Tables 2.3 and 2.4 in Chapter 2 which highlight the sectors dominated by small manufacturers and independent retailers. The potential agent can then seek out suitable manufacturers in two ways:

1. Buy the relevant trade journals, eg for textiles the *Draper's Record* or *Knitting and Haberdashery Review*. If he doesn't know what the

journals are, he can look them up in *BRAD* (*British Rate and Data*) which lists all publications by trade sector and can be found in large public libraries and the libraries of colleges of higher education and polytechnics. Advertising agencies also have copies of *BRAD* and may allow you to consult it.

2. Join the MAA and read its monthly magazine for the advertisements. It would be wise to join the MAA in any case for guidance in drawing up contracts, especially for someone with no previous experience of working as an agent.

Most self-employed agents are paid through commission on sales which can very from about 5 to 20 per cent, depending upon the product sold.

The Manufacturers' Agents Association is located at 1 Somers Road, Rcigatc, Surrcy RH2 9DU; 0737 241025.

British Agents Register (BAR)

BAR operates in the same field as the MAA and, like the latter organisation, it offers guidance on agency agreements and contracts as well as a service designed to match agents and manufacturers.

The annual registration fee is £38. In addition, the member can purchase a *Handbook for the Manufacturer's Agent* and the *Guide to Agency Agreements and Contracts*, each costing £6. If he pays by standing order the annual registration fee is £35. Upon joining, the agent is entered on a register which classifies him in two ways:

The area(s) he covers
The types of outlet on which he calls.

A separate register is kept for technical agents. Any principal who is seeking an agent is sent details of registered agents who meet his requirements. Among the many organisations advertised as having found agents by these means are BBC Industries, Hambro Life, Cuprinol, and United Parcels. The service appears to be actively marketed judging by the speed with which the author's enquiry was handled and the volume of publicity material subsequently received. In addition, the registered agent receives a monthly magazine called *British Agents Review*. The July 1989 edition contained an interesting article on the ingredients required for a successful agent/manufacturer relationship in addition to over 40 advertisements from organisations seeking agents. The products involved ranged from babywear and hygiene equipment to automotive test equipment, reinforced plastic pipes (for a German company) and mobile telephones. BAR believes that a high proportion of agency posts are not advertised at all but are filled by use of this register.

A person thinking of becoming an agent could use the BAR in the same way as the MAA described above. The BAR can be contacted at 24 Mount

Parade, Harrogate, North Yorkshire HG1 1PB; 0423 560608.

The International Commercial Network, based at the same address as BAR, offers established agents the opportunity to obtain details of international trading opportunities through a publication called *Worldwide Marketing Opportunities Digest*. This costs £75 for two years.

Franchising

Franchising is an increasingly popular way of starting a business. As many books and articles have been written about it, I will deal with it briefly, though there is more information on specific franchises in Chapter 10.

I refer throughout to *business format* franchising in which franchisees trade under the name of a franchisor. It offers many of the advantages of self-employment and reduces many of the risks. The franchisor owns a tested item of commercial value – usually a brand name and/or product or service such as Dyno-Rod, Body Shop or British School of Motoring – which he allows someone else, the franchisee, to use. The franchisee pays the franchisor for the right to use his name, usually in the form of a royalty payment related to sales. The franchisee benefits from the experience, training and advertising of the franchisor and keeps any profits he makes after paying royalties. The franchisor benefits because he can expand his business more rapidly by using the franchisee's capital and the latter's commitment to making money for himself. For this reason, franchises are believed to be particularly appropriate to organisations involving much personal contact with the public, such as restaurants. Good service, patience and good humour come more easily, especially on wet days in Wigan, when the franchisee's livelihood depends upon them than they do when the only motivator is a remote head office who probably don't even know the names of the humbler staff in the branch.

A survey in 1988 estimated that business format franchising accounted for sales of almost £4 billion is Britain through 16,000 outlets employing over 180,000 people. In the USA franchising accounts for a much larger proportion of business than in Britain where, however, it is growing rapidly. The large and well-known franchise organisations such as Wimpy and Prontaprint have hundreds of franchisees while smaller and newer enterprises may have only one or two.

It is impossible to estimate accurately the total number of business format franchise organisations currently operating, since many of them are small and local and virtually anyone can start one with very little formality. However, the list of members of the British Franchise Association (BFA) is a good guide to the structure of the industry. The BFA has at present about 90 full members. To achieve full membership franchisors are required to submit a completed application form to the BFA which includes a copy of their prospectus, their franchise agreement and some financial information. They must also demonstrate that they have successfully operated a pilot scheme for at least one year, financed and managed by the applicant company. In addition, they have to produce evidence of successful franchising over a subsequent two-year period involving at least four franchisees.

The present membership includes a number of very well-known companies, like Alfred Marks and Avis, as well as a number of less well-known organisations. The BFA also has almost 30 associates who, like the full members, have to demonstrate that they have run a pilot scheme successfully for at least one year. They must also provide evidence of successful franchising for one year with at least one franchisee. Associates are also accepted if they are substantial organisations with more than 25 company-owned outlets, even if they do not have franchisees in operation at the time of application. The BFA was formed in 1976 with the aim of ensuring good practice and ethical behaviour in the establishment of franchises. They have a number of publications designed to advise both potential franchisors and franchisees and they can be contacted at Thames View, Newtown Road, Henley-on-Thames, Oxfordshire RG9 1HG; 0491 578049.

The most common categories for franchise operations are services, retailing and fast foods. Services include business services (eg the Accounting Centre); cleaning services (Molly Maid); and despatch (Interlink Express Parcels). Building and maintenance services are particularly well represented by organisations like Drips Plumbing, Kwik Strip and Dyno-Rod. Retailers include Tie Rack, Foto Inn, and a number of convenience stores including Late Late Supershop and Circle K. Fast-food outlets like Perfect Pizza, Spud-U-Like and the Pancake Place are prominent in the list of franchises in the catering industry. Motor vehicle franchises include well-known names like Budget Rent a Car. There are also franchise opportunities in printing (eg Prontaprint and Kall-Kwik) and in beauty and health care such as the Body and Face Place.

A disadvantage to the franchisee is that anyone can set up as a franchisor with no guarantee of competence or good character. For this reason it is essential to check out not only the credentials of someone offering a franchise but also the profit potential that he may be claiming for his idea. The latter may owe more to wishful thinking than to hard achievement. There are several ways of checking someone out. First, there are several excellent books on the subject. *Taking Up a Franchise* by Colin Barrow and Godfrey Golzen (Kogan Page, £8.95) and *The Good Franchise Guide* by Tony Attwood and Len Hough (Kogan Page, £19.95) are excellent guides to the subject and include lists of franchise opportunities currently being offered with a brief description of each and an indication of the investment required. The BFA has several excellent publications including *How to Evaluate a Franchise* by Martin Mendelsohn which costs £5.95.

In addition to this background research you can check out the franchisor's claims by speaking to some of his existing franchisees to find out how successful they have been. Ask for a list of franchisees and then choose one or two yourself. If you go to see the ones which are chosen for you by the franchisor, it is likely that he will send you to those who have been successful. You need to see the others as well. Ask to see their accounts. As indicated earlier, if the franchisor is a full member of the BFA he must have at least four franchised outlets and if he is confident about his claims he will be glad for you to speak to them. If the franchise is a new one and has not yet had time to establish a track record then you should be very cautious about proceeding unless you are sufficiently familiar with the business proposed to be able to judge its prospects from your own experience.

Some of the saddest tales in franchising concern people who have gone into franchise businesses of which they had no previous experience, lured by promises of high earnings. You are much more likely to make a success of running a pizza restaurant if you have previously worked in the catering field than if you have just left a job as a technician in the RAF. The learning process in any new business is bound to be long and expensive and some people never recover financially from the experience. If, on the other hand, you already have some knowledge of the business that you are going into, possibly through previous employment, then much of your learning has already been completed. One guide to the value of a franchise is the number of people whom the franchisor rejects. It is estimated that, on average, one in 14 applicants for franchises survives the vetting procedures applied by franchisors. The rest are rejected either because they lack the resources or they have the wrong experience. If you find that a franchisor is too eager to accept you into his organisation it may be an indication that you would be better off out of it.

If you check out a franchise opportunity in the ways described, you should be able to eliminate the worst risks and find a franchise which is best suited to your experience and resources. You also have the reassuring knowledge that you are adopting a business idea which has been tested by someone else, and found to work. The franchisor will be anxious for you to succeed and will give you the benefit of his knowledge and experience to ensure that you do. For these reasons, franchised outlets are less likely to fail in the early stages than businesses started without the benefit of this prior experience. This fact is also recognised by the banks who view franchisees as promising candidates for loan finance. All the major clearing banks have appointed franchise managers whom you should contact via your local branch or via the small business sections of the major banks whose addresses are given in Chapter 9.

Summary

A wide variety of franchise opportunities is available to people with some capital to invest, quite small sums being required in some cases. Finance is also available from banks. The risk of business failure is reduced by taking a franchise with a proven record and this can usually be checked out without too much difficulty.

CHAPTER 4

Licensing Opportunities

Many opportunities exist throughout the world for companies to market products or services which have been developed by other organisations who are in no position to handle them with their own resources. Several organisations exist to publicise and promote these enterprises and some of them are described in this chapter. Generally speaking, these opportunities are of a kind which would be best suited to an existing organisation seeking opportunities to diversify or expand.

International Licensing

This is a monthly publication produced by International Licensing Ltd of 92 Cannon Lane, Pinner, Middlesex HA5 1HT; 081–866 2812. The annual subscription is £40. The journal consists mainly of short notices describing new products and processes which are available for licensing, often for foreign companies who wish to market internationally. US-based companies are a major contributor but many others are represented including Britain, France and Germany. The May 1989 issue contained over 100 notices covering a wide variety of products (with the country of origin) including:

Hovercraft for emergency and rescue operations (USA)
Diesel exhaust gas cleaning system (Germany)
Infant and juvenile wooden furniture (USA)
Disposable paper briefs (Canada)
Sportswear (USA)
Non-stick coating (France)
New manufacturing process for lightweight, knocked down furniture (USA).

This journal would be of value to an established business, large or small, seeking new products or processes for its range. Most of the notices concern technical products or processes although a few have a direct application in consumer markets like some of those mentioned above.

British Technology Group (BTG)

British Technology Group claims to be the world's leading technology transfer organisation. BTG licenses new scientific and engineering products to industry worldwide and provides finance for the development of new technology.

Technology transfer
BTG's aim is to promote the commercial use of new technology arising from research at UK public sector sources such as universities, polytechnics, research councils and government research establishments. BTG takes responsibility for protecting the inventions concerned, seeks licensees and negotiates licence agreements with industrial companies. Its net revenue is shared with the source on an agreed basis. Many inventions require further development before being licensed to industry. BTG provides finance for development, usually to the organisation at which the initial research was carried out.

Finance for innovation
As part of its technology transfer role BTG can also offer finance to companies that want to develop new products and processes based on their own technology. Through its industrial product finance scheme, BTG can provide up to 50 per cent of the funds required for the development and launching of a new product and will expect to recover its investment by means of a percentage levy on sales of the resulting product or process. The subsidiaries of foreign-owned companies are eligible for BTG finance provided that the resulting business will be located in the UK.

Start-up companies
Where a particular technology requires the setting up of a new company, BTG can perform a catalytic role in promoting the creation of start-up companies. For further information on British Technology Group, please contact: Head of Marketing, BTG, 101 Newington Causeway, London SE1 6BU; 071–403 6666.

World Business Publications

World Business Publications Ltd is a British organisation which publishes a series of monthly reviews drawing attention to opportunities in the marketing and technical fields. It publishes six journals, each appearing monthly, of which four are briefly described below. The purpose of each publication is to inform companies in the relevant fields of the existence of new technologies and ideas. In some cases, the companies concerned will wish to purchase the products for their own use. In others, more relevant to this context, they represent licensing opportunities for organisations who have the resources to manufacture and/or market the products concerned. The main sources of the ideas included in the publications are described as:

> Government departments
> Research institutes and universities
> Trade fairs
> Chambers of Commerce
> Subscribers to the journals.

World Trade Link: The Monthly Review of New World Trading Opportunities

This is divided into 15 product classifications ranging from foodstuffs and beverages to paper, electrical equipment and furniture. The July 1989 edition contained several hundred entries by organisations either wanting to sell or seeking distributors for a diverse range of products. A few examples are bridal accessories; industrial floorings; textile printing machinery; perfumes. The cost of an annual subscription to *World Trade Link* is £124.50.

Technology Transfer International

The July 1989 issue contained descriptions of over 30 technical innovations, seeking licensing or co-operation agreements. These are almost by definition high-tech and range from robotic wrists and rolling mills to lozenges against dental plaque. The cost of a year's subscription is £152.

New Coatings and Surfaces

This publication is aimed at people in the coatings and surfaces industry who wish to be kept informed of technical developments, many of them offering licensing opportunities. The May 1989 issue contained about 50 entries including a special section on patents. Products come from all over the world and range from chrome plating to special coatings for the Concorde aeroplane when flying at supersonic speeds. A year's subscription costs £156.

World's New Products

The July 1989 edition contained descriptions of almost 200 new products from all over the world in categories ranging from pharmaceuticals, food and textiles, to building materials, electronic equipment, transportation, instrumentation and sports equipment. Many of them are highly technical but they include Japanese canoes, South African home exercise systems, an American motorised golf bag and a blisterproof sock! A year's subscription costs £147.

For details of these and other publications write to: World Business Publications Ltd, 960 High Road, London N12 9RY; 081–446 5141.

International New Product Newsletter

This organisation, based in the United States, produces a number of publications in the new product field of which the most interesting is the *Venture/Product Digest*. This publication developed from an earlier one produced by the American company, General Electric (GE), which originated in GE's desire to market products developed by its own research and development departments but which the company did not wish to manufacture itself – perhaps because they were too small or in a market which GE did not wish to enter.

Venture/Product Digest is now published by a separate organisation and covers a much wider range of activities than those of GE itself. Other corporations, universities, government departments and research institutions worldwide are contacted for suitable products and processes. The products featured range from highly technical ones such as fuel cell modules and ceramics to boat bumpers and a video device designed to keep children entertained in supermarkets – the latter from an organisation based in Great Britain. Each write-up in the *Digest* gives the name of the new product or process, a description of how it works, its advantages and marketing potential and the name and address of contacts for licensing purposes. The annual subscription is $120. For further information write to: International New Product Newsletter, Box 1146, Marblehead, Maryland 01945, USA.

Technology Exchange

The Technology Exchange was founded by its present managing director, Brian Padgett, in February 1986 as an organisation devised to assist smaller firms to take part in new product licensing. The company is a non-profit distributing organisation formed to help those who seek new business opportunities through licensed manufacture, distribution agreements, joint ventures or company purchase. It is supported by a number of large companies and public bodies.

Four times a year it publishes a catalogue called *Technoshop* for which the annual subscription is £40. The spring 1989 catalogue consisted of 36 pages and about 180 product entries. The database of licence opportunities currently contains some 14,000 items with 200 new opportunities being added each week. The catalogue is prepared with small firms in mind and the following will give some indication of the contents:

> *Sportswear*. A French manufacturer of sports clothing in a range of styles, materials etc, seeks a UK distributor and/or partner for cross-marketing.
>
> *Computer diskette storage carousel*. Patent/manufacturing licence offered for a plastic storage carousel.
>
> *Taxi radio manufacturing*. A small business located in Wales manufacturing a taxi radio system is offered for sale at £50,000.
>
> *Knitwear products*. Joint venture sought by Irish manufacturer of high quality hand loom knitwear.

For further information on the activities of the Technology Exchange, please write to: Brian Padgett, The Technology Exchange Ltd, Wrest Park, Silsoe, Bedford MK45 4HS; 0525 60333.

Summary

There are abundant opportunities for companies to enter into licensing agreements to manufacture or market products. Many of these are highly technical and best suited to large, technologically sophisticated organisations. However, as has been shown, this does not apply in every case and some organisations, notably the Technology Exchange, specialise in providing a service which would be of value to small organisations seeking to diversify, or in a few cases, to experienced individuals seeking to start their own businesses.

CHAPTER 5

The Idea Sellers

Several books and periodicals are published offering ideas and opportunities for starting or expanding businesses. The quality varies greatly, as does the price, and the price is not always a guide to quality. Some publications from Britain, the USA and France are reviewed here.

Great Britain

Periodicals
A firm very active in the field of generating business ideas is Chartsearch Ltd, which has an annual turnover of approximately £7 million. A substantial proportion of this is in business opportunity periodicals and publications, though the company also publishes periodicals which advise on investments.

Chartsearch's longest running publication in the business opportunity field is called *Business Opportunities Digest*. It is published monthly at an annual subscription of £39.50 for the first year and £59.50 for subsequent years. It consists of 16 A4 pages with a substantial editorial content containing information of interest to the small business. The June 1989 edition, for example, contained information on various ways of securing funds for investment, small business competitions, how to recruit staff and how to get the best out of your accountant. It also contained information on useful publications and forthcoming television programmes which would be of interest to the small business.

However, the most interesting part of the publication in the present context concerns the short case studies of people who have set up in unusual businesses. These are often businesses which are confined to a small area, so the opportunity, by implication, exists for others to start similar businesses elsewhere. A typical edition contains about 20 such ideas and the June 1989 issue included a person who had set himself up as an antiques headhunter, finding specific items for clients; a company established to produce videos of houses for estate agents which has become very successful as a result of making use of the advice of the Small Firms Service (see Chapter 9); a packing and mailing service started up by a housewife for small companies who thereby do not need to stock a wide variety of packaging materials; and an accommodation/forwarding address business started by a housewife to serve busy executives and others who are frequently absent from home for long periods and need to have important mail dealt with.

Chartsearch also publishes many books on business opportunities, far too numerous to mention here. Some of these books cover a wide variety of business opportunities and others focus on specific enterprises – for example, desktop publishing or mail order selling. For further information about all Chartsearch publications, please write to them at 14 Willow Street, London EC2A 4BH.

Business Head Start

This publication appears six times a year. It costs £19.50 for a trial subscription and £34.50 for an annual subscription. A sample copy costs £5 and annual subscribers also receive a free book called *Lucrative Sideline Opportunities* describing a number of business ideas. The circulation claimed is approximately 7000. It contains editorial material of interest to small businesses, a number of short case studies of successful businesses which may be emulated elsewhere and some pages of advertisements, mostly concerned with business opportunities. A recent issue described the experience of a training consultant, with information on how he set up and obtained his clients; a photographic business which specialises in pictures for glossy advertising brochures, magazines and posters; a packaging consultancy; and a computer consultancy. There is also a section on market gaps and novel products, some of them offering opportunities to potential distributors. These include waste compactors, a seat belt cutter for fast release in an emergency and a watch which talks!

For further information about *Business Head Start* write to them at 6 May Court, Nottingham NG5 2BG.

Books

There are innumerable books on small business. Most of them are concerned with the process of establishing a business – company formation, VAT registration, finding an accountant etc – once the business idea has been found, and they deal briefly if at all with the task of finding a good business idea. A typical example is *Starting a Successful Small Business* by MJ Morris (Kogan Page, £6.99) which has recently gone into its second edition.

However, a number of publications contain useful sections on finding suitable products or ideas. *Making Money Part-Time* by Alan and Deborah

Fowler (Sphere, £3.95) contains a wide variety of ideas from candle-making to street vending which should help you to think imaginatively, though if you wish to pursue the ideas further you will need more details than the book contains on each idea. *Going Freelance – A Guide to Self-employment with Minimum Capital* by Godfrey Golzen (Kogan Page, £7.99) describes a variety of ideas in rather more detail, though you will still need to do more research if you wish to embark on any of them. Finally, *Running Your Own Mail Order Business* by Malcolm Breckman (Kogan Page, £6.99) contains an excellent section on finding interesting and unusual products for a mail order business if this is what interests you.

All the above titles can be ordered through good bookshops but a number of titles in this field can be obtained only if ordered direct from the publishers. This applies to Chartsearch publications mentioned above, and also to a similar range of business opportunity books published by Bookworm Publications of Tynygroes, Conwy, Gwynnedd LL32 8BR.

Some books which purport to offer ideas for making money are so trite that they invite burlesque. One, whose publicity made particularly extravagant claims, contained fewer than 100 pages of text and cost £12.50 plus postage and packaging. Most of the content was devoted to exhortation and hyperbole of the most naive kind including the claim that gross profit was in the region of 150 per cent, though the arithmetical basis of this astonishing achievement was not made clear. Reputable mail order publications offer a refund to dissatisfied purchasers and you should be cautious of ordering books from mail order sellers who do not include an assurance of this kind in their advertisements.

The United States of America

The Entrepreneur

The Entrepreneur magazine is published monthly, annual subscription $49.97 from the subscription department, 2392 Morse Avenue, PO Box 19787, Irvine, California 92713–9441. It is aimed at existing and aspiring entrepreneurs and consists of about 100 pages, about 40 per cent of which are devoted to advertisements.

The advertisements commonly include business books and services together with a substantial number for businesses, distributorships and franchises. The magazine includes features on franchising and new business ideas. There are interesting articles on attracting venture capital, government support for business in the USA and lots of tips on selling, promotion etc. Despite the euphoric style of many of the advertisements, the magazine contains much valuable information and advice and many short descriptions of business ideas, some of which would no doubt transfer successfully to the UK. However, market conditions in the USA can vary greatly from those which apply in the United Kingdom and it does not follow that an idea which has succeeded in America will succeed here. Moreover, it is particularly difficult to evaluate the success of a product in the USA, as distinct from the claims made by its proponents, since it is almost certainly impractical for you to research the market on the spot. For this reason, the ideas promoted in the *Entrepreneur* should be treated with caution.

France

Some of the most interesting publications that I have encountered are to be found in France. Unfortunately, none of them is published in an English language version so you have to make the effort either to translate them yourself or to persuade a friendly linguist to do so for you. Most of these publications are on display in a specialist book shop in Paris called *Le Salon Permanent des Idées d'Affaires*, situated at 23 rue des Apennins, Paris 75017. The nearest Metro station is Brochant and the shop is within easy walking distance of Montmartre.

One of the publications available from this address is called *Job Pratique*, a magazine which appears every two months at a cost of F25. Each issue contains ideas on setting up businesses and case studies of existing successful businesses – for example, a framing service. This magazine is published from the same address as the Salon itself.

A second organisation, whose publications are available there but which is based elsewhere, is called Editions Selz, based at 43 Grand Rue, 68000 Colmar, France. You can contact them by dialling 010 331 89–24–04–64. They publish a magazine which appears every two months called *Idées Lucratives* (Profitable Ideas). The annual subscription is F790 – about £80. Each edition includes two substantial features, examining in some depth two business ideas. Each is covered in some 20 to 30 pages. There are several shorter articles, one to five pages long, featuring new ideas and successful businesses, and some pages of book reviews and miscellaneous features. Recent editions have included long features on running a flea market, opening a computer shop and organising exhibitions.

About 80 back numbers of *Idées Lucratives* are available to subscribers at any one time although the list changes continually as it is updated. These single editions cost F245 – about £25 each. For a current list with prices and synopses, please write to Editions Selz at the address above if you are unable to visit the Salon in Paris.

A third publication on sale is called *Défis – Créer Son Entreprise*. This costs F18 and appears each month. It contains a good selection of case studies of successful new enterprises together with advertisements for business opportunities and franchises. Among the ideas featured in a recent edition were: a low-cost journal, launched by two journalists for people in the 13–16 year age group; and a home catering service specialising in Chinese food.

The publications listed, which are selected from many others available in the Salon, will give some idea of its character. I would not suggest that you should make the journey specially to Paris to visit it but if you are there for other reasons you are not likely to see, elsewhere, so many business ideas gathered under one roof. The Salon is open from Monday to Friday, 10.00 to 12.30 in the morning and 2.00 to 5.15 in the afternoon. If you are visiting Paris in August, it is best to telephone beforehand to make an appointment since many staff are on holiday at that time and the shop is not always open as advertised. However, if you let them know in advance that you are coming they will open specially for you as they did for me. The telephone number from the United Kingdom is 010 331 42–28–59–00.

'Loadsamoney'

As an author of books and newspaper articles on small business, my name finds its way on to numberless mailing lists which are used by people who wish to sell me business ideas. It is not too difficult for me now to recognise those which are long on hype and short on genuine value. Some of them I throw away. Some of the more exotic ones I put into a file marked 'Loadsamoney' and use the contents to warn others who may be taken in by the promises they make. Occasionally, I am so outraged by the claims that I complain to the Advertising Standards Authority. I give below a few examples of the kind of material which you should treat with great caution.

One of my most persistent correspondents was a gentleman in a remote part of the kingdom who claimed to hold a senior military rank and made several attempts to offer me an infallible system for betting money on horses. By paying him £25 I could be sure of learning a secret that would enable me to become a millionaire. I imagine that such offers have been made since Roman times and I am sure that the only people who make any money out of them are those who are selling the so-called systems. I complained to the Advertising Standards Authority about the activities of this gentleman since I am sure that many people are taken in by it, but it is extremely difficult for the ASA to control individuals who are sending such material through the post. The ASA cannot stop someone posting a letter.

A second mail shot offered me the opportunity to make a great deal of money by selling products which would restore people's vitality, virility and hair! I am sure that if such a product existed it would make a great deal of money for someone. In fact, the Advertising Standards Authority Code of Practice specifically forbids advertising of this kind and when I complained to them they were able to prevent further use of this mail shot since the person sending it out was part of a large organisation which should have known better.

Other similar material has held out to me the chance of becoming a millionaire; offered me the world's most powerful money manual; and invited me to enter a booming business that never falters. Recently, I have noticed an increase in the number of organisations which offer me the opportunity to make a fortune by entering various lotteries. The most remarkable of all offered me the most important money/power/ romantic love discovery since the Industrial Revolution for a little more than £50.

Other opportunities include the sale of exotic underwear and 'fun products' (the imagination boggles at what they are!) and various cosmetic preparations which are designed to restore the most unpromising material to health and vitality.

I am sure that many people waste small sums of money on offers of this kind and I occasionally meet more tragic cases of people who have lost far more than they could afford. The only safe advice is to insist on seeing the product before you pay any money. If the vendor has a product or idea which he genuinely believes to be of value, he will not mind showing it to you and answering your questions about it. All the others should be treated with the suspicion that they deserve.

Summary

There is a very wide variety of business opportunity material available. Some of it is interesting and useful; some of it is worthless. If you are thinking of purchasing any books, publications or other materials, it is best to see them before you part with any money. Some of the products are available only by mail order but in this case the journals in which the advertisements are contained nearly always insist that the purchaser be given the opportunity to claim a refund within a certain period if he or she is not satisfied with the goods. If this offer is not contained in the advertisement then I would strongly advise you against purchase. The more reputable organisations are only too happy to let you see their merchandise. They know that if you are satisfied with what you buy from them there is a good chance that you will purchase from them again.

CHAPTER 6

Sources of Information for Evaluating Your Business Opportunity

The previous chapters have been concerned with identifying those activities in which small businesses have a reasonable chance of success. However, it does not follow that they will succeed regardless of circumstances. Most florists, as we have seen, are independent businesses but to be successful a new florist must be opened in the right kind of area and not too close to the competition. This does not preclude the competition moving in later. The least you should do is enquire at your local authority planning department to see if they know of any proposals for opening other businesses similar to yours in the area. See also Chapter 7 for methods of measuring the value of an existing business.

This chapter describes sources of information, readily available in good libraries, which will enable the entrepreneur, at little expense, to make a realistic assessment of the chances of success. Research will greatly reduce the chances of costly failure later. There is an almost infinite variety of sources of information when researching business opportunities and the following criteria have been applied before including such sources here.

1. The publications are available in good public libraries or those of polytechnics, colleges and business schools which normally allow access to people from the local community. In other cases they are available at moderate cost or, in a few cases, free.
2. They are comprehensible to the layman who is prepared to take a little trouble. They do not require specialist knowledge or a grasp of technical terms.

3. They are pointers to other sources (eg through cross-references)
    which the investigator may use if he or she wishes.

Government statistics

The government statistical service publishes an infinite variety of data on
every aspect of our national life. Many of their publications have been used
in preparing this book and they are referred to in the text. The most useful
are mentioned below; they should be available in a good public library and
are sold by the government book shop, HMSO. *Guide to Official Statistics*
(latest edition, £21.95) is the basic reference work which will guide you to
the main sources of data which interest you. The *Annual Abstract of Statistics*
(1989, £18.50) is a summary of the government's statistical publications and
it is valuable, not only for its information, but also for its helpful reference
to its sources which can then be easily traced.

The results of some government enquiries are not always published as
annual digests but as summaries. Particularly commended is *Social Trends*
(1989 edition, £21.95) which gives summary information on population
trends, education, employment, income, health, housing, leisure and many
other activities. In many cases the information is imaginatively presented
with charts and graphs being used in place of tables.

Finally, for anyone thinking of opening a shop, *Business Monitor SDA 25
Retailing Enquiry* published every two years (latest edition, £15) contains
detailed information on retail trades, trends, market share of independents
etc. It also shows what the gross profit levels are for different types of
retailer (ie sales less cost of goods sold) which is a useful guide to the level
of profit you can generate to cover your overheads. This is a figure you
should be familiar with if you are thinking of buying a business in case the
person selling the business to you tries to overstate the gross profit levels.

Census of Population

A full copy of the latest (1981) *Census of Population* is found in large
public libraries. The volumes covering your local area are also likely
to be held in your branch library. Intelligently used, they can provide
you with significant local information. One set of volumes deals with
Key Statistics for Urban Areas and another set deals with each county
separately.

Key Statistics for Urban Areas – Cities and Towns contains the following
data:

Table 1   The total population for each town broken into males and females.
Age groups, with a further male/female split for pensioners.
Percentage of population originating in new Commonwealth, Pakistan or Eire.

> *Example of use*: anyone thinking of setting up a business dependent upon one of these groups (eg a children's clothing shop, an old people's home or an 'ethnic' food shop) could estimate the relative market potential in a number of towns in a region.

Table 2   Classifies the population in each town by:
Social class.
Proportion with higher education qualification (with male/female split).
Industry of employment – seven categories.

> *Example of use*: a bookseller could compare the social class and higher education profile of neighbouring towns, since these both affect the demand for books.

Table 3   Economic activity and unemployment, with a further breakdown by men, married women and single, widowed or divorced women.

> *Uses*: a general indicator of the level of prosperity in an area; also to show potential demand for a service specifically for unemployed people, eg cheap TV hire.

Table 4   Household tenure, amenities and cars. For each town it shows:
Proportion of owner-occupiers; private rented; council tenants.
Number of rooms per household.
Proportion of households with no car; one car; more than one.

> *Uses*: this table is another indicator of prosperity. A decorating business should know which towns are dominated by owner-occupiers rather than tenants. A driving school needs to know the proportion of households with cars.

Table 5   Size and types of household; pensioners; children; and travel to work methods.
Average number of persons per household.
Proportion of single-person households (pensioners and non-pensioners shown separately).
Proportion of households with two or more pensioners and no one else.
Proportion of households with six or more people.
Households with one, two, three or more children.
Method of travel to work: bus, rail, car, on foot.

Uses: services aimed specifically at pensioners (perhaps a tea-room or social centre) or at families with children (a nursery school or pizza restaurant) can use this data to compare neighbouring towns. A newsagent, before opening or buying a station kiosk, would need to know which towns have heavy commuter populations.

Five regional volumes of *Key Statistics for Urban Areas* are published, as well as a summary volume for Great Britain. The regional volumes cover smaller towns as well as the larger ones included in the national summary.

County Reports

These are similar to the urban area reports but go into considerably more detail. There are separate entries for each local authority area with a very detailed age split, in five-year bands, with children under 16 broken down into one-year bands. Birthplaces of heads of households born outside the UK are divided into more categories – Caribbean, India etc. There is more detailed classification of occupation and of household tenure and house size. A much more detailed profile of economic activity in the county is held on microfiche. The population is broken into 160 occupations, with information about whether they live or work in the counties. Information in this detail could be used to supplement that on urban areas which has already been described, perhaps by a business contemplating a service aimed at a very specific group, for example an executive luncheon service for senior management and professional people.

Companies House

Companies House, at 55 City Road, London EC1Y 1BB; 071–253 9393, holds copies of the annual report and accounts of every limited company registered in the UK, from ICI to your local greengrocer (if the latter is a limited company). Copies of the report and accounts on microfiche can be obtained by callers at a cost of £2.50 each or by post at £5.50 each from Companies House, Crown Way, Maindy, Cardiff CF4 3UZ; 0222 388588. Microfiche readers are available in Companies House itself and in most libraries. The accounts tell you, among other things, annual sales, gross profit, overheads and net profits.

The net profit figure is not very helpful with small, owner-managed companies since accountants do many clever and legitimate things with writing-down allowances, leases, owners' drawings etc to minimise taxation. However, if you can obtain the accounts of two or three businesses trading in the same market as yourself and in a similar town they should give you a rough idea of the turnover and gross profit you can eventually expect. If, for example, you know you need £20,000 gross profit to cover your overheads and your own salary and you find that similar businesses in comparable towns cannot manage to do this, then it is best to know before you sign the lease.

Industrial training boards

There are eight training boards and, besides running courses for the industries they serve, they also carry out research into those industries which can provide valuable background material. Material from the Hotel and Catering Industry Training Board has been used in the preparation of this book. You can contact the boards at the following addresses:

Agricultural Training Board
32–34 Beckenham Road, Beckenham, Kent BR3 4PB; 081–650 4890

Clothing and Allied Products Industry Training Board
80 Richardshaw Lane, Pudsey, Leeds LS28 6BN; 0532 393355

Construction Industry Training Board
Dewhurst House, 24 West Smithfield, London EC1A 9JA; 071–489 1662

Engineering Industry Training Board
PO Box 176, 54 Clarendon Road, Watford WD1 1LB; 0923 38441

Hotel and Catering Industry Training Board
International House, High Street, Ealing, London W5 5DB; 081–579 2400

Plastics Processing Industry Training Board
Coppice House, Halesfield 7, Telford, Shropshire TF7 4NA; 0952 587020

Road Transport Industry Training Board
Capitol House, Empire Way, Wembley, Middlesex HA9 0NG; 081–902 8880

Man Made Fibres Industry Training Advisory Board
40 High Street, Rickmansworth, Hertfordshire WD3 1ER; 0923 778371

If you write to any of these boards, they will send you a list of their publications for sale.

National Economic Development Council

This body, commonly known as Neddy, was established 27 years ago as a forum in which government, industry and the trade unions could discuss and plan the economy. Its interest for the small business lies in the activities of some of its subcommittees which carry out research into the future prospects and needs of individual industries. Recent work includes, for example, studies of opportunites for import substitution in clothing and footwear and the future of town centres as shopping areas.

The publications are reasonably priced and a full catalogue of them (called 'NEDO in Print') can be obtained by writing to the National Economic Development Office, Millbank Tower, Millbank, London SW1P 4QX; 071–217 4037.

Marketing Pocket Book

This useful little guide is published by the Advertising Association, Abford House, 15 Wilton Road, London WC1V 1NJ; 071–828 2771. It costs £12.50 (1990 edition) and comprises 120 pages of facts and figures about consumers, the economy, channels of distribution, advertising expenditure, the media and other aspects of marketing. A number of definitions which are useful to the layman are included; for example, it defines the mysterious, A, B, C1, C2, D, E social grades which are more often referred to than understood. It gives information on market values (did you know that we spend £7 million a year on garlic to the distress of our fellow travellers on the underground?) and it tells you how many people buy the *Sun* (4,219,000) and *the Transformers* (64,821) where a full-page ad in the company of the exotic products of science fiction will cost you £700. The book is particularly good at referring to its sources. This is a valuable and entertaining little book for someone thinking of starting out on market research for the first time.

Mintel Publications

This company is based at 18–19 Long Lane, Barbican, London EC1A 9HE; 071–606 4533 and 6000, and started up in 1972. It produces monthly digests, known as 'Mintel Reports', each one containing reports on about five different markets such as DIY, skincare preparations, books. Some of the information is taken from existing publications, including government sources, and some is produced by Mintel from its own surveys. The current (1989) annual subscription to Mintel is £590. The cost of a single issue is £145. Mintel also produce separate reports on retailing, leisure, personal finance and European markets and special studies of individual markets. The reports are very useful summaries of information on a wide variety of consumer markets and should not be neglected by anyone thinking of entering a market, particularly if he or she is unfamiliar with it. The reports normally contain some views on the direction the market is taking and factors to consider when entering it. Recent issues which could be of interest to people thinking of starting in business are:

September 1989:   Health food shops
                                   Bicycles
August 1989:   Carpets and floor coverings
July 1989:   Pizza
                                   Employment intermediaries

If you wish to see a Mintel publication then there is some guidance at the end of this chapter on libraries you should approach.

Euromonitor Publications

Euromonitor, based at 87–88 Turnmill Street, London EC1M 5QU; 071–251 8024, produce a monthly digest called *Market Research Great Britain* (*MRGB*) which is similar to the Mintel monthly report. For example, in October 1985 they produced a report on the market for bread which would be of interest to anyone opening a bakery since it drew attention to the rapid growth of the wholemeal sector in the face of an overall decline in bread consumption. The annual subscription to *MRGB* is £295 (1989). A single copy costs £60. They produce a monthly report on European markets and special reports on a variety of markets. These studies have included franchising, retailing and health foods.

Yellow Pages

Yellow Pages not only lists all the traders with a business telephone number in a given area, it also enables the user to perceive which towns are well supplied with a certain service and which are poorly supplied, thus giving a first indication of market gaps. Every trader with a business telephone qualifies for a free entry and a few pay extra for a bold or display advertisement. The local area directory is delivered free to all telephone subscribers in the area and a copy is also to be found in the local library which normally also stocks directories for surrounding areas. Larger libraries hold the complete set of 65 volumes which cover the United Kingdom.

Businesses are subdivided into about 3000 classifications ranging from abattoirs to zoos. It is possible, by making use of the information, to calculate which communities are well supplied and which are poorly supplied with the kind of business you are thinking of starting. One would expect neighbouring towns with similar populations and similar socio-economic profiles to be equally well supplied with certain services such as bookshops, restaurants and other facilities which predominantly serve a local market. Taken in conjunction with the other sources mentioned they can give a preliminary idea of the most promising location for the business you have in mind.

Intelligent use of the sources described (and of others you will come across as the work proceeds) will reduce the chances of your making costly mistakes. Chapter 8 illustrates how this can be done, taking as examples four activities which are often associated with small firms.

Libraries

Many of the publications referred to in the text are expensive and the reader may wish to see copies of the material before deciding which to buy. Most public libraries have a selection of books on small businesses, but if you are looking for the specialist market reports referred to in this chapter, you are more likely to find them in large or specialised libraries.

Foremost is the Science Reference Library at 25 Southampton Buildings, Chancery Lane, London WC2 1AW. This is a public reference library near Chancery Lane station, and is open all day Monday to Friday as well as Saturday morning. Major public libraries in large cities (for example, the Central Library, Manchester) and the libraries of about 30 polytechnics and colleges running courses in management, marketing or business studies, also hold a good selection of this material. If you approach the librarians of these institutions they will almost invariably welcome your enquiry and allow you to consult the material in the libraries themselves. It is usually not possible even for students to take these publications out of the library since they are valuable and in constant use but this should not be necessary since it should be perfectly possible for you to extract the necessary information by working in the library itself.

CHAPTER 7

How Much Does it Cost?

The cost of becoming established in a business will vary enormously with the type of activity involved. If your business is selling a service which you will provide personally (for example, as a management consultant or bookkeeper), then your setting-up costs will be virtually nothing if you work from home. If your service requires some equipment, such as a car for a manufacturer's agent or a word processor for a secretarial service, then it is fairly easy to assess the costs of purchasing or leasing these items.

Other home-based businesses may require more outlay on facilities and working capital than is at first apparent. It is commonly believed that working as a self-employed agent or representative involves little or no overheads. In fact, anyone operating on this basis will require a good car which will incur substantial running expenses as it is in constant use. In addition, it is likely that the representative will incur bills for hotels and meals when staying away from home if he or she is covering a wide area as is commonly the case. These costs tend to be disregarded by employees since they are met by the employer but they amount to a significant overhead for the self-employed person.

An executive catering service run from home on any but the smallest scale needs food preparation and storage facilities which are larger and more sophisticated than those required for normal domestic use and may require an investment measured in thousands of pounds. Many small decorating and building businesses are run from home and these can require substantial storage facilities for equipment and, particularly, for materials. Bricks, cement, timber and ladders occupy a lot of space and much of it has to be under cover. For this reason small builders often find themselves in dispute with neighbours and with local authorities for conducting from their homes trading activities which are offensive to their neighbours. These problems can be overcome by hiring suitable premises such as garages or small warehouse units.

However, most businesses eventually require investment in premises, materials and equipment. The purpose of this chapter is to give some idea of the costs of becoming established in businesses of the kind mentioned earlier in the book and examples are given of the prices of some businesses which are currently (1989) being offered for sale. I am indebted to Mrs Pamela Henson of the Tring office of Lakey & Co for much of the information provided in this chapter.

Sources of finance

You first need to establish what finance is available to you. This is likely to come from three sources:

1. Any *cash* or *cashable assets* you have, for example savings; redundancy payment or golden handshake; investments in bonds, shares or other securities which can readily be converted to cash. This 'cash' element normally represents a fairly small proportion of the finance potentially available to an individual.

2. *Property*. You may be a householder in a dwelling worth £80,000 on which you have a mortgage of £30,000. In this case your share of the house (often referred to as your equity in the house) is worth £50,000 and you could realise this investment if you chose by selling the house and paying off the mortgage, leaving you with £50,000 to invest in your business in addition to the cash described in 1 (above). Selling your home to start a business might be regarded as risky but it is an action you might consider if the business premises themselves provide living accommodation such as a dwelling space above the shop or workroom.

3. *Loans*. Banks and other institutions will normally make loans which are secured against the assets of the business you are buying. If you are purchasing a business with a freehold property then a loan can normally be obtained of up to 65–70 per cent of the total purchase price, excluding stocks, with the freehold property in effect mortgaged to the lender as security. On a leasehold concern the loan is unlikely to exceed 50 per cent of the purchase price, excluding stock. In either case the lender (eg a bank manager) will only make the loan if he believes, after examining your business, that it will generate sufficient income for you to repay the loan and interest.

What the price includes

Having looked at these three sources of finance you should have a rough idea of the level of investment you can make. You now have to ask what it is that you are paying for when you buy a business. Normally, you pay for at least four things:

Premises

You buy the right to occupy the premises from which the business is conducted. This may mean purchasing the freehold outright, ie actually owning the property; or it may mean purchasing the leasehold interest which entitles you to rent the premises for a defined period, usually with an option to renew.

If you buy a business in a freehold property then the property element is likely to constitute by far the greatest proportion of the purchase price. You have the security of an investment in the property and, as indicated earlier, you will be able to raise a substantial loan by mortgaging it. However, you will need far more money for a freehold than for a leasehold. For example, a newsagent whose value as a business is £20,000 (see below for business valuation) may be trading from premises which, as an empty building, would be worth £80,000, so to purchase the business with the freehold would cost you £100,000.

This is an option you might consider if you are going to live 'over the shop' and are in effect buying a home for £80,000 and a business for £20,000. However, it means that most of your money is invested in bricks and mortar and only a small proportion in the business itself. This is the reason that most businesses are leasehold. The freehold is normally owned by an insurance company, a property company or some other organisation which sees itself as being in the property business. The trader buys a leasehold interest in the building at a fraction of the cost of buying the building itself. This means that the trader can use his funds to do what he is best at – selling books, making toys etc – and does not have his precious capital tied up in bricks and mortar.

Sometimes traders who own freeholds sell them to a property company, lease them back for a small proportion of the selling price and use surplus funds to expand their businesses. A well-known supermarket chain did this 'sale and leaseback', as it is called, a few years ago to finance the opening of some new hypermarkets. The main disadvantage of a leasing arrangement is that you will have to pay rent and this will be subject to review – nearly always a euphemism for an increase. In the examples of the cost of buying a business given later in this chapter, I have clearly indicated which businesses are freehold and which leasehold.

Tools of the trade

The second element in the cost of buying a business lies in the 'tools of the trade' – the fixtures and fittings, specialised machinery and other essential items of equipment. In the case of a retail business these are likely to be a small proportion of the total cost, rarely exceeding a few thousand pounds and sometimes amounting only to a few hundred. In the case of a manufacturing or service business employing specialised equipment such as machine tools or computers this is likely to account for a substantial proportion of the cost. In a business like a restaurant which requires substantial investment in kitchen equipment, tables, chairs etc, you are likely to buy them much more cheaply in an existing restaurant than they would cost you new from the manufacturers, since the value of such equipment second-hand on the open market is much less than as new.

Stock

The third element in the purchase price of a business is the cost of stock, that is to say the saleable goods owned by the business when you buy it. This is *not* normally included in the quoted purchase price of a business although it is likely to be quite important in the case of a retail business. The reason it is not included is that the value of stock varies from month to month. A business with £10,000-worth of stock when you first see it advertised for sale may have only £6000-worth when it is sold two months later. Businesses are therefore normally advertised for sale at a quoted price 'plus sav' which means 'stock as valued'. On the day you take over, the stock is valued according to a procedure you have agreed (eg by professional independent stocktakers at cost price) and this is what you pay.

You need to allow for investment in stock in your calculation of the capital you require. The accounts of the business you are buying should show you the value of their stock at year end. You can cross-check these figures by looking at industry norms, published in government statistics. For example, if you are thinking of buying a women's clothing shop then Table 3 of Business Monitor SDA 25 *Retailing Enquiry* shows that the ratio of sales turnover to year-end stocks in such businesses in 1982 was 5. In other words, a business with sales of £50,000 had stocks of £10,000 at the year end. The latter figure is likely to be lower than the stock levels for much of the year since many companies choose to end their year at a time when stocks will be low in order to make stock-taking easier. By making calculations of this kind and allowing for error you can estimate the amount of working capital you will need for stock.

Track record

The fourth element in the purchase price of a business is its track record: the loyalty of its customers, its reputation in its chosen field and above all its prospects of earning profits in the future for its new owner. This is often referred to as its 'goodwill'. A small business with a modest turnover and few tangible assets but which consistently earns good profits is more valuable to its owners than a larger business with shining new equipment but a long record of losing money.

The prospects of future profits are what should really interest you when you buy a business. They are also the most difficult to measure and predict of the four elements. The prospects of future earnings should strongly influence the purchase price of the business and this should apply whether it is a billion-pound conglomerate which is the subject of a city take-over battle or the sale of the local newsagents. The assessment of a company's prospects is based essentially upon two factors: its recent track record and any likely future changes.

The first, its recent track record, can be assessed by examining its annual accounts, preferably with the professional help of an accountant or other expert in business valuation. When judging a privately owned company on its accounts in this way, however, certain factors which differentiate them from large public companies should be borne in mind. The latter, generally speaking, like to maximise their declared profits in order to please shareholders. Private companies, who have to please no one but their owners, can adopt a number of perfectly legal devices to minimise taxable profits and thus reduce the burden of tax. Skilful use of capital allowances and leasing arrangements can achieve this. So can more unconventional means. If a local newsagent chooses to deliver newspapers to outlying areas in a custom-built Ferrari which the business has bought for the purpose this will certainly affect the level of profits. It will probably also lead to a prolonged and lively correspondence with the Inland Revenue!

An experienced accountant should be able to adjust the accounts for you to allow for factors like this and arrive at a reasonably clear picture of the business's record. This should also help you to see through any sudden improvements in a business's fortunes. Beware of businesses which, after years of poor profits, suddenly see a dramatic improvement in performance just before being offered for sale. I cannot emphasise too strongly the importance of obtaining professional advice in evaluating a business, particularly if it is one of which you have little or no experience. Remember that the person selling the business to you wants to present it in the most favourable light and you cannot blame him for doing this. You must insist on seeing sales and profit figures for the most recent trading period and if these are not available, for whatever reason, you should suspect the worst.

Predicting likely future changes is more difficult but even more important. A business can turn in a steady profit for years and then collapse because a large chain store opens a competitive outlet a few doors or streets away. The wise owner sells the business before the collapse begins but do not let him sell it to you! It is worth spending time looking at the neighbourhood, reading local newspapers and enquiring of the local planning authority to establish whether major developments of this kind are planned.

On the other hand, look out for ways in which you can realistically hope to improve the business. An acquaintance of mine had the opportunity to purchase a decaying neighbourhood grocery store at a low price which reflected its performance. He discovered that there was nowhere within two miles that the population could buy newspapers or alcoholic drinks. He contacted a newspaper wholesaler who said he would supply him. (This is important since wholesalers limit the number of newsagents in an area to ensure a reasonable throughput for each – hence the popularity of newsagents shops as small businesses.) He bought the shop, added newspapers and frozen foods and obtained a liquor licence. The turnover doubled in six months. He had turned it from a grocer's into a convenience store.

The premium you pay for a business's goodwill will vary according to its transferability. If you buy a sub-post office and general store which can be run by you just as efficiently as by a former owner you may pay a fairly high premium for the goodwill – perhaps three times the annual profits. If you buy a business with a strong element of personal service such as a hairdresser's you cannot expect to command the loyalty of the customers which the previous owner has built up over many years. You should therefore pay a much more modest premium for the goodwill.

Businesses for sale: some examples

The following are examples of businesses offered for sale in autumn 1989 in Hertfordshire, Bedfordshire and Buckinghamshire. Some are freehold and in this case the cost of the business will reflect the high property values prevailing in southern England. For further information on similar businesses in the area, please write to Lakey & Co, 49 High Street, Tring, Hertfordshire HP24 5AG.

Annual sales and gross profit levels quoted (where available) are taken from the prospectuses. From gross profit must be deducted overheads such as rent, heat, light, staff wages etc, to give net profit which is, in effect, the salary before tax of the owner. It would be wrong to judge the relative value of businesses by comparing the gross profits. A small toy shop may generate far less gross profit than a cafe. However, the toy shop may occupy a small secondary site with low rent and rates, and have no wages bill at all. A cafe is likely to occupy a much more expensive site and to employ far more staff, especially if it offers waitress service. This information should be evident from the accounts when you see them. The first figure quoted is the asking price for the business. For convenience I have divided the businesses for sale into five categories.

Food retailing
£39,950 Licensed delicatessen/continental general stores
Leighton Buzzard; Turnover £2500 per week; Gross profit 35 per cent; 15-year lease.

£175,000 Village post office/licensed general stores
Mid-Bedfordshire; Turnover £111,138; Gross profit £19,655; Post office
salary £6200; Three-bedroomed accommodation; Freehold.

£12,950 Greengrocers
Stevenage; Turnover £800 per week; Gross profit 30 per cent; Leased to
year 2000.

£38,000 Fruit, vegetables and flower shop
Stevenage; Turnover £2200 per week; Gross profit 34 per cent; seven-year
lease.

£29,950 Greengrocers
Luton, Bedfordshire; Turnover £2200 per week; Gross profit 33 per cent;
eight-year lease.

£39,950 Village butchers
St Albans; Turnover £2500 per week; Gross profit 30 per cent; 14-year
lease with three-bedroomed maisonette.

£235,000 Freehold off-licence with separate video shop
Watford area; Turnover: Off-licence £168,459; Videos £37,000; three-
bedroomed accommodation; Freehold.

Clothing/Footwear
£39,950 Childrenswear shop
Harpenden, Hertfordshire; Turnover £87,000; Gross profit 47 per cent;
Leasehold.

£27,500 Well-established menswear shop
Watford; Turnover £75,000; Gross profit 42 per cent; 12-year lease.

£14,950 Wool and fabric shop
Ampthill, Bedfordshire; Turnover £20,363; Gross profit 50 per cent;
Leasehold.

£37,500 Menswear shop
South Bedfordshire; Turnover £63,000; Gross profit 40 per cent; 12-year
lease.

£189,000 Shoe shop
Bedfordshire; Turnover £149,000; Gross profit 30 per cent; Freehold.

£24,000 Shoe shop
Tring, Hertfordshire; Turnover £88,000; Gross profit 40 per cent.

Other retailers
£100,000 Two retail TV and hi-fi shops
Buckinghamshire/Hertfordshire; Turnover £415,000; Gross profit 24 per cent; Leasehold.

£58,500 Newsagents
Hertfordshire village; Turnover £2400 per week; Gross profit 19 per cent; three-bedroomed maisonette included; 15-year lease.

£95,000 China tableware
Watford; Turnover £3000 per week; Gross profit 50 per cent; two-bedroomed flat included; three-year lease.

£35,000 Games software unit
Letchworth, Hertfordshire; Turnover £1000 per week; 12-year lease.

£175,000 Jewellers
Watford; Turnover £85,029; Gross profit £41,911; two/three-bedroomed flat included; Freehold.

£65,000 Newsagents
Hertfordshire; Turnover £3200 per week; Gross profit 20 per cent; Leasehold.

Catering businesses
£45,500 Workingmen's Cafe
Bedfordshire/Buckinghamshire border; Turnover £1000 per week; Leasehold.

£95,000 Licensed restaurant
Hertfordshire village; Turnover £2000 per week; Gross profit 60 per cent; Leasehold.

£49,950 Italian restaurant
Dunstable; Turnover £87,103; Gross profit 50 per cent; Leasehold.

£115,000 Fish and chip shop
Mid-Bedfordshire village; Turnover £1800 per week; Gross profit 64 per cent; Freehold.

£33,950 Tea-room/cake shop
Bedfordshire; Turnover £45,000; Gross profit £20,380; one-roomed accommodation; Leasehold.

£75,000 Fish and chip shop
Bedfordshire; Turnover £1500 per week; Leasehold.

£79,950 Sandwich bar
Luton; Turnover £2000 plus per week; Gross profit 65 per cent; Leasehold.

£75,000 Fish and chip shop
Bedfordshire; Turnover £800 per week; Gross profit 60 per cent; Freehold.

£15,000 Catering service (catering for dinner parties)
Hertfordshire; Turnover £40,000; Gross profit 75 per cent.

Miscellaneous businesses
£25,000 Hairdressers
Bedfordshire; Turnover £33,420; Leasehold.

£29,950 Car valeting service
Bedford; Turnover £750 per week; Gross profit 75 per cent; Leasehold.

£19,950 Paint stripping and architectural salvage business
Hertfordshire; Turnover £24,000; Gross profit 70 per cent.

£245,000 Printing business
Bedfordshire; Turnover £112,000; Gross profit 54 per cent; includes freehold element of the industrial unit.

£59,950 Wholesale suppliers of florist sundries
Bedfordshire, Buckinghamshire, Hertfordshire area; Turnover £158,226; Gross profit £29,937; Operating from vendor's home as a cash and carry van delivery service.

The above figures are not intended as a guide to the true value of the business though they do illustrate the wide variations in turnover and gross profit between different types of business, ranging from less than 20 per cent for a newsagent to 75 per cent for catering establishments. You and your advisers would have to make your own assessment of the value of the business to you. The figures are simply an indication of the order of investment required for businesses of different sizes and types.

CHAPTER 8

How to Research a Business Opportunity

This chapter takes a small business idea from each of the sectors described in Chapter 2 and shows how each idea may be assessed, using mainly the sources of information mentioned in Chapter 6 or elsewhere in this book. The sectors and examples are:

Manufacturing – a small bakery
Retailing – a bridal boutique
Catering – a vegetarian restaurant
Services – an old people's retirement home

A Small Bakery

We have seen in Chapter 2 that bread and flour confectionery is a field in which 13 per cent of jobs are in units of fewer than ten people (twice the national average for small units), so clearly it is a field in which there is a place for small firms.

First, we need to know something about the market for bread and pastries. A report in *Market Research Great Britain* in October 1985 showed that, while consumption of bread per person has almost halved in the last 30 years, causing one major manufacturer to withdraw from the market altogether, there has been a dramatic increase in the consumption of wholemeal and wholewheat bread. A Mintel report in November 1988 estimated the value of the market for bread as £1.58 billion in 1987 and confirmed that over the five-year period 1983–87 consumption of bread had continued to decline from 30.8 to 30 oz per person per week. However, it also revealed that the decline was confined to the white bread sector which accounted for over half of total consumption. Consumption of brown bread was increasing but the real growth was in the wholemeal sector which increased from 2.7 to 4.7 oz per person per week during this period. The same report showed that wholemeal bread is consumed primarily by ABC1s (the *Marketing Pocketbook* should be consulted for definitions of these

73

categories) and the report concluded that this sector will continue to grow and that many consumers will continue to be attracted by products which are free of additives and preservatives. There is much other information in this Mintel report which would be invaluable to a person who was thinking of starting a small bakery.

Having obtained an overall picture of the market you are thinking of entering you now need to learn where to locate your business, bearing in mind that you would benefit from serving an area with an above average proportion of ABC customers. According to the *Marketing Pocketbook* these comprise 39 per cent of the population. Using the *Census of Population – Key Statistics for Urban Areas* we can ascertain which towns have the highest numbers of these groups. The social grades used in the census are slightly different from the ABC groups but very easy to relate to each other using the definitions given. Yellow Pages will reveal how many bakers already operate in the area and, if you are thinking of opening a bakery unit as part of a retail outlet, it will also tell you how many retail bakers there are. A visit to them will ascertain whether they are already providing the kind of service you have in mind.

If you feel that there is a market gap, then use Yellow Pages for another area to find two or three businesses similar to your own but distant enough to be non-competing. Contact the owners, tell them what you are thinking of doing and ask if you can visit them. Write first so that they know where you are or they may suspect that you are opening up next door! Most people enjoy talking about their businesses and are flattered when someone seeks their advice. The author has only ever once been refused an interview.

Obtain a copy of the annual report (if it's a limited company) and encourage the owners to talk to you about turnover, gross profit, suppliers (good and bad) and customers. You will probably learn, for example, that the customers include several restaurants and executive dining rooms as well as housewives, since Mintel estimates that 15 per cent of bread consumption lies outside the home. You will probably also learn that some suppliers are legendary for poor service and that some products are much more seasonal than you thought. Having completed this process you now know:

1. Who your customers are:
    ABC1 groups
    Restaurants etc.
2. Which towns in your area contain the largest number of these potential customers.
3. What the competition is.

From these three facts, you should be able to choose the best location. Finally, by comparing your chosen location with those of the companies you have approached, you should be able to make an estimate of your turnover and gross profits. This will be only an approximation, but much better than a guess, and it will certainly please your bank manager when you ask him for some money. One of the most interesting business case studies I have ever examined was that of a small independent bakery started up in an Oxfordshire village by a vegetarian guitarist producing delicious bread, cakes and pastries which were free of additives and preservatives. Within a year the business was generating sales of £75,000 per annum and had secured a contract to supply one well-known supermarket group and the food hall of a world famous London department store.

You may, of course, conclude that you have no chance of success. It is far better to reach that conclusion before committing your savings to a hopeless enterprise.

A bridal boutique

This example has been chosen because many of these outlets are opening, sometimes two or three in a small town. The overheads associated with such an enterprise are substantial if it is based in a retail unit and it is essential to establish that the potential market will justify these fixed costs. First, you need to know the size of your potential market which will of course be determined by the number of weddings. *Social Trends* (1989 edition, Table 2.12) shows that each year there are about 260,000 first marriages and about 138,000 in which one of the partners has been married before. With a population of just under 57 million this equates to one first marriage for every 219 people plus one remarriage for every 413 people. We shall concentrate on the first marriages because they are most likely to be 'white weddings' of the kind for which bridal boutiques are designed.

It can easily be calculated that, in a town of 15,000 people, there would be 15,000 divided by 219 marriages in a year = 68 marriages. Since women are more likely to undergo first marriages when they are in their twenties than at any other time (*Annual Abstract of Statistics*, 1989, Table 2.5) the boutique owner will want to know whether her town is well or poorly populated by this age group. She can check this by looking at the *Census of Population – Key Statistics for Urban Areas* which gives an age breakdown of the population which she can compare with the national average. If she lives in a new town she may find that the proportion of 20-year-olds is 50 per cent higher than the national average, in which case, in the town of our example, there would be about 100 weddings a year. In Eastbourne, with a high proportion of elderly people, there would be fewer. A visit to the local churches or registry office will confirm or modify her calculations and give some information on seasonality (March to June is the most popular time) and the average number of bridesmaids (about two). From this she can calculate the total potential market. However, even if offered the opportunity to dress half the weddings in her market area, she might be unable to cope if too many came within a short period.

Next, she needs to know what competition she has. This information is in Yellow Pages under 'Wedding Services' though it would not include dressmakers working from home without a business telephone. For this she should consult the advertisements in the local press, including parish magazines.

By contacting one of the bridal chains such as Pronuptia, the franchise organisation, she can learn about the capital required (£20,000–£40,000) and profit margins. By visiting a non-competitive outlet in a similar town at a safe distance she can obtain some idea of the number of garments she can hire or sell each year, and the gross profit.

She now has the following information:

1. Total market size:
    100 weddings using 100 brides' dresses and 200 bridesmaids' dresses.
2. Likely market share:
    Using information from the non-competitive outlet: allowing for home dressmaking etc, she would do very well to capture half the market even in the absence of other bridal boutiques.
3. Estimated sales, calculated by multiplying the total market by the estimated share.
4. Gross profit.

She can use the information she has obtained about overhead costs from non-competitive outlets to see whether her gross profit is adequate to cover her costs and leave a reasonable remuneration for herself.

A vegetarian restaurant

The Mintel report for December 1987 contained a feature on health food shops which estimated that there are between 1 and 2 million vegetarians in Great Britain. In 1985, a Mintel special report on healthy foods and health foods included further information on the age and socio-economic profiles of people using health foods.

Vegetarian restaurants are still comparatively rare in Britain, but a careful perusal of Yellow Pages will reveal enough of them for you to visit so that you can assess the kind of food they offer and the customers they attract. One of the better known ones is called Food for Friends situated in Brighton which was featured in *Venture Capital Report* in February 1985. It is also written up as a case study in *Routes to Success* (Kogan Page, 1986). From these sources you can obtain information about the origins of the business and its founder, together with a sample menu and the interesting information that the great majority of the customers are not vegetarians but are attracted by healthy food at reasonable prices.

There is a detailed profit forecast for two years including projected sales and gross profit levels. Finally, the French organisation Idées Lucratives (see Chapter 5) produced in 1983 a dossier on vegetarian restaurants which gave information on the market (in France of course), setting-up costs and profit projections.

A venture into a field as new and untested as a vegetarian restaurant is bound to be riskier than entry to a more familiar field, but since the direct competition is correspondingly less the possibilities of higher rewards are also great if the right formula is found. Even in a market as obscure as this one, it is possible, using the four sources suggested, to increase significantly the chances of success by understanding the customers, the products and the basic economics of the operation. Finally, the Hotel and Catering Industry Training Board provides booklets on setting up a restaurant, recruiting and training staff etc.

An old people's retirement home

In Chapter 1 it was suggested that trends in the age structure of the population can create needs and therefore opportunities. Of particular note is the substantial increase forecast in the number of people aged 85 and over. The *Census of Population* will tell you how many elderly persons are resident in each town/district, how many live alone and what kind of housing and amenities they have – owner-occupied, rented, with or without bath etc. The local social services department will be able to advise you which types of accommodation for elderly persons are in short supply – sheltered housing, retirement homes, nursing homes.

Provision can range from accommodation, meals and care in a converted private home for two or three elderly persons to full nursing care for the chronically sick. In certain circumstances, the local authority will pay for the cost of accommodating elderly persons and the social services department will tell you about this.

The regulations governing the provision of elderly persons' accommodation are complicated, but you can find out about these by obtaining a copy of *Home Life: A Code of Practice for Residential Care* which is published by the Centre for Policy on Ageing, 25–31 Ironmonger Row, London EC1V 3QP; 071–253 1787. The Director of Social Services at your County Hall also publishes a guide on residential care for the elderly setting out regulations and guidelines on such matters as room size, access, staff/resident ratios and amenities.

Summary

Any business venture involves a degree of risk and the possibility of failure can never be entirely eliminated. In Great Britain each year almost £200 million is spent on market research. Nearly all of this is spent by large organisations looking for opportunities in the market-place and identifying the qualities that would minimise the risk of failure. This chapter shows that small organisations venturing into unfamiliar fields can achieve the same results by taking some trouble and putting imagination and intelligence to work on information which can be obtained at little cost.

CHAPTER 9

Existing Help for Small Business

Following the 1971 publication of the Bolton Report, many schemes have been established to help small businesses start up or expand. Judging from the rapid expansion in the number of small firms noted in Chapter 1, they have met with considerable success. The main schemes are as follows:

Government-funded schemes

The Small Firms Service
This was established as a result of the recommendations of the Bolton Report. Until 1985 it was part of the Department of Trade and Industry. In autumn 1985 it was moved, together with its Minister, to the Department of Employment – a reflection of the importance the government attaches to small firms as job creators. It acts as the focus for all government policy and activity in support of small firms and operates through a network of regional offices in major towns. It is the first point of contact for anyone seeking advice on start-up, expansion or any other matter concerned with small firms.

The offices can be contacted by asking the telephone operator for Freefone Enterprise. Local offices can help the small businessman in two ways. First, they can direct him to whichever agency can best help with his particular need, for example to an enterprise agency, a bank, or a training programme, all described below. Second, they can put him in touch with a small firms counsellor. These are usually retired or semi-retired businessmen who cither have experience of running a small firm or have occupied senior posts in large firms. They include accountants, engineers, retailers, marketers etc. They act, in effect, as consultants to businesses which are starting up, wishing to expand, or running into difficulties. They occasionally complain that they are called in to advise firms on how to extract themselves from problems which would not have arisen if they had been consulted earlier, for example before starting up.

In 1988, 529 small business counsellors were working for the Small Firms Service in England and in the year 1987–88 they handled 39,138 counselling sessions involving 27,359 small firms. These resulted from 266,174 enquiries to Small Firms' regional offices in that year. The client is entitled to three counselling sessions free of charge with the Small Firms Counsellor after which he is expected to pay £30 a day. The Small Firms Service also publishes a number of brochures for small firms on a range of subjects – starting up, exporting, staff recruitment and training etc – and these are available from regional offices.

The headquarters of the Small Firms Service is now at the Department of Employment, Steel House, Tothill Street, London SW1H 9NF; 071–273 3000. You will be put in touch with your local office if you dial the operator on 100 and ask for Freefone Enterprise. The addresses of regional offices are:

Birmingham
9th Floor
Alpha Tower
Suffolk Street
Queensway
Birmingham B1 1TT
021–643 3344
Covering: Coventry, Hereford, Shropshire, Staffordshire, Warwickshire, West Midlands MBC, Worcestershire

Bristol
6th Floor
The Pithay
Bristol BS1 2NB
0272 294546
Covering: Avon, Cornwall, Devon, Dorset, Gloucestershire, Somerset, Wiltshire

Cambridge
Carlyle House
Carlyle Road
Cambridge CB4 3DN
0223 63312
Covering: Cambridgeshire (inc Isle of Ely, Huntingdon, Peterborough), Norfolk, Suffolk

Cardiff
16 St David's House
Wood Street
Cardiff CF1 1ER
0222 396116
Covering: the whole of Wales

Glasgow
21 Bothwell Street
Glasgow G2 6NR
041–248 6014
Covering: Scotland

Leeds
1 Park Row
City Square
Leeds LS1 5NR
0532 445151
Covering: Yorkshire and Humberside

Liverpool
Graeme House
Derby Square
Liverpool L2 7UJ
051–236 5756
Covering: Merseyside and Chester

London
Ebury Bridge House
2–18 Ebury Bridge Road
London SW1W 8QD
071–730 8451
Covering: Greater London, Kent,
Middlesex

Manchester
26–28 Deansgate
Manchester M3 1RH
061–832 5282
Covering: Cheshire, Cumbria,
Lancashire, Greater Manchester,
Derbyshire, (High Peak District) and the
Isle of Man

Newcastle
15th Floor
Cale Cross House
156 Pilgrim Street
Newcastle Upon Tyne
NE1 6PZ
091–232 5353
Covering: Cleveland, Durham,
Northumberland, Tyne and Wear

Nottingham
Severns House
20 Middle Pavement
Nottingham NG1 7DW
0602 481184
Covering: Nottinghamshire,
Derbyshire
(excluding High Peak District),
Leicestershire, Lincolnshire and
Northamptonshire

Reading
Abbey Hall
Abbey Square
Reading RG1 3BE
0734 591733
Covering: Berkshire, Oxfordshire

Stevenage
Business and Technology Centre
Bessemer Drive
Stevenage
Hertfordshire
SG1 2DX
0438 743377
Covering: Bedfordshire,
Buckinghamshire, Essex and
Hertfordshire

DTI – The Department for Enterprise

The DTI's Enterprise Initiative has been heavily advertised on television and in the press but it is not always fully appreciated that much of the effort is aimed specifically at small firms. In particular, the programme has a series of consultancy initiatives offering, in effect, subsidised consultancy of a very high quality which is designed to enable small firms to improve their management in a number of key areas. Firms with fewer than 200 employees qualify for assistance. The schemes are managed on behalf of the DTI by organisations which are experienced in the field. The schemes are described below.

The Marketing Initiative

The Marketing Initiative, managed for the DTI by the Chartered Institute of Marketing, will help small firms to develop an overall marketing strategy for the home or export markets. An expert consultant will advise the client on changing market needs, pricing, after-sales service or any changes in the product mix that may benefit from changes in the environment such as the Single European Market. The aim of the Initiative is to enable small companies to develop sophisticated and effective marketing plans.

The Business Planning Initiative

This Initiative is managed for the DTI by 3i Enterprise Support Ltd, an organisation with extensive experience of investing in small growing companies. A consultant will help the firm to analyse its business and markets and establish clear objectives and strategy.

The Financial and Information Initiative

This is also managed by 3i Enterprise Support Ltd and will help small firms to develop financial and information systems to provide information on resources, production, customers and competitors, making use of information technology where appropriate.

The Quality Initiative

This is managed for the DTI by the Production Engineering Research Association and, in the North West, by Salford University Business Services Ltd. This offers expert advice on the introduction of quality management systems which meet the appropriate standards – national or international – for your kind of business.

The Design Initiative

This is managed by the Design Council and offers consultancy on product innovation, design for production, performance and reliability, materials selection, packaging and other design-related elements.

The Manufacturing Initiative

This is managed for the DTI by the Production Engineering Research Association and offers expert advice on manufacturing strategy and helps to introduce modern methods and systems.

In the case of each of these Initiatives, the DTI will pay half the cost of between five and 15 man days of consultancy. In assisted areas and urban programme areas, DTI will pay two-thirds of the cost. For details of these areas see below. For further information about the Consultancy Initiative consult the nearest regional office of the DTI whose addresses are given below.

Regional enterprise grants also apply in the development areas and South

Yorkshire. Under this scheme, businesses employing fewer than 25 can obtain regional enterprise grants of 15 per cent of the cost of plant and equipment up to a maximum grant of £15,000; and up to 50 per cent of the costs of improving products or processes or developing a new product. In this case the maximum grant is £25,000. The regional offices of the Small Firms Service can act as contact and referral points for these DTI Initiatives. Alternatively, you may wish to contact your local DTI office direct in which case please contact the addresses and telephone numbers listed below. If you are in any doubt about which regional office to contact, then telephone the freephone number 0800 500 200 and ask for the booklet called *DTI – The Department for Enterprise – A Guide for Business*. The regional offices with the first contact point are as follows:

DTI North East
Stanegate House
2 Groat Market
Newcastle upon Tyne
NE1 1YN
091–232 4722

DTI North West
75 Mosley Street
Manchester M2 3HR
061–838 5000

DTI Yorkshire and Humberside
Priestley House
Park Road
Leeds LS1 5LF
0532 443171

DTI East Midlands
Severns House
20 Middle Pavement
Nottingham NG1 7DW
0602 506181

DTI West Midlands
Ladywood House
Stephenson Street
Birmingham B2 4DT
021–631 6181

DTI South West
5th Floor
The Pithay
Bristol BS1 2PB
0272 272666

DTI South East
Bridge Place
88/89 Eccleston Square
London SW1V 1PT
Main contact point for Consultancy
Initiatives 071–627 7800

DTI South East also has several regional offices whose telephone numbers are as follows:

Cambridge 0223 461939	Chatham 0634 828688
Chelmsford 0245 492385	Ipswich 0473 210611
Margate 0843 290511	Norwich 0603 761294

Portsmouth 0705 294111   Reading 0734 395600
Reigate 0737 226900

DTI Scotland   **DTI Wales**
Alhambra House   The Welsh Office Industry Department
45 Waterloo Street   Cathays Park
Glasgow G2 6AT   Cardiff CF1 3NQ
041–248 2855   0222 823 185

Export Marketing

If you work for small organisation which wishes to develop its export marketing then your normal first point of contact for the Export Initiative should be your DTI regional office (details above). However, the DTI has special contact points for certain issues and the most important of these for small firms are given below:

Small Firms Issues
071–215 5485 or 071–215 4770

Export Marketing Information Centre
The DTI has a wealth of information which can help you to research your most suitable export markets and for this you should telephone 071–215 5444.

Special Areas

Special areas of the United Kingdom (usually those associated with high levels of unemployment) qualify for higher levels of government assistance than others. As indicated in the previous section on the various Enterprise Initiatives, the DTI can pay half the cost of five to 15 man days of consultancy but in assisted areas, this figure can rise to two-thirds of the cost. Your regional office of the DTI will be able to advise you on whether you are located within the boundaries of one of these areas. The following list is a rough guide to their location.

England

North West   **North East**
Accrington and Rossendale   Bishop Auckland
Blackburn   Darlington
Bolton and Bury   Durham
Liverpool   Hartlepool
Part of Manchester   Middlesbrough
Rochdale   Morpeth and Ashington
Widnes and Runcorn   Newcastle upon Tyne
Wigan and St Helens   South Tyneside
Wirral and Chester   Stockton-on-Tees
Workington   Sunderland

Yorkshire and Humberside
Barnsley
Bradford
Doncaster
Grimsby
Hull
Rotherham and Mexborough
Scunthorpe
Sheffield
Whitby

South West
Bodmin and Liskeard
Bude
Cinderford and Ross-on-Wye
Falmouth
Helston
Newquay
Penzance and St Ives
Redruth and Cambridge
Plymouth

East Midlands
Corby
Gainsborough

West Midlands
Birmingham
Coventry and Hinckley
Dudley and Sandwell
Kidderminster
Telford and Bridgnorth
Walsall
Wolverhampton

Wales

Aberdare
Bangor and Caernarfon
Bridgend
Cardiff
Cardigan
Ebbw Vale and Abergavenny
Fishguard
Flint and Rhyl
Haverfordwest
Holyhead
Lampeter and Aberaeron

Llanelli
Merthyr and Rhymney
Neath and Port Talbot
Newport
Pontypool and Cwmbran
Pontypridd and Rhondda
Porthmadog and Ffestiniog
Pwlheli
South Pembrokeshire
Swansea
Wrexham

Scotland

Alloa
Ayr
Arbroath
Badenoch
Bathgate
Campbeltown
Cumnock and Sanquhar
Dumbarton
Dundee
Dunfermline
Dunoon and Bute
Falkirk
Forres
Girvan
Glasgow
Greenock
Invergordon and Dingwall
Irvine
Kilmarnock
Kirkcaldy
Lanarkshire
Lochaber
Newton Stewart
Skye and Wester Ross
Stewartry
Stranraer
Sutherland
Western Isle
Wick

Isles of Scilly

Enterprise Zones

In addition to the development areas, Enterprise Zones are areas specially designated by the Department of the Environment to promote industrial and commercial investment. This is achieved by relaxing planning procedures, by exempting organisations from local authority rates for a ten-year period, and by certain tax concessions. The Enterprise Zones are listed below but they do not necessarily cover the whole area concerned. You should enquire of your local authority where the boundaries are or write to the Department of the Environment, 2 Marsham Street, London SW1P 3EB; 071–212 7158.

England	*Wales*
Corby	Delyn
Dudley	Milford Haven
Dudley (Round Oak)	Swansea
Gateshead	
Glanford (Flixborough)	*Scotland*
Hartlepool	
Isle of Dogs	Clydebank
Middlesbrough	Glasgow
Newcastle	Inverclyde
North-east Lancashire	Invergordon
North-west Kent	Tayside
Rotherham	
Salford Docks	*Northern Ireland*
Scunthorpe	
Speke (Liverpool)	Londonderry
Telford	
Trafford Park	
Wellingborough	
Workington	

The Rural Development Commission (RDC)

The Rural Development Commission was until recently called the Council for Small Industries in Rural Areas or CoSIRA, a name by which it is still commonly known. It is responsible to the Department of the Environment. Its priorities are 'rural regeneration and development through a service to small firms in the country areas of England'. The RDC provides this service to manufacturing and service firms, village shops and post offices, rural transport businesses, and tourism and leisure businesses in certain areas. Any such firms employing 20 skilled persons or fewer may apply to the RDC for assistance. The Commission has about 300 full-time and 70 part-time staff who work from a head office in Salisbury and regional offices throughout England. Similar functions in Scotland and Wales are performed by the local development boards described later.

The RDC staff offer a range of services designed to stimulate industry and employment in rural areas which are normally defined as communities with a population under 10,000. First, it offers advisory services on business management – bookkeeping, marketing etc. It operates a most active engineering project development workshop and a full build and design service. Second, it offers a wide range of courses both in business management and individual crafts – engineering, forge work, thatching, pottery, saddle making, glass etc. It also publishes books on these subjects.

The Commission runs a financial service which includes a close working arrangement with the four major clearing banks and a loans service of its own. Loans may be made towards the cost of land purchase, building work, equipment and the working capital requirements of businesses. Assistance is also given in the preparation of business plans, which may be used to support applications for finance and contribute towards the long-term planning of the business itself. A high proportion of clients applying to the regional offices of the RDC do so because they are wishing to start businesses. The following are the RDC's local offices. You should use them as your first contact point if you wish to seek help.

North Region

Northern Regional Office
Ullswater Road
Penrith
Cumbria CA11 7EH
0768 67294

12 Churchfield Court
Barnsley
South Yorkshire
S70 2JT
0226 204367

Morton Road
Yarm Road Industrial Estate
Darlington
County Durham DL1 4PT
0325 487123

14 Market Place
Howden
Goole
North Humberside DN14 7BJ
0430 431138

Northumberland Business Centre
Southgate
Morpeth
Northumberland NE61 2EH
0670 511221 or 514343

Ullswater Road
Penrith
Cumbria CA11 7EH
0768 65752

15 Victoria Road
Fulwood
Preston
Lancashire PR2 4PS
0772 713038

William House
Shipton Road
Skelton
York Y03 6XW
0904 646866

West Region
Western Regional Office
Strickland House
The Lawns
Park Street
Wellington
Telford
Shropshire TF1 3BX
0952 57400

6 Shropshire Street
Audlem
Cheshire CW3 0DY
0270 812012

Stanley House
47a High Street
Henley in Arden
Solihull
West Midlands B95 5AA
0564 24191

32 Church Street
Malvern
Worcestershire WR14 2AZ
0684 564784 and 64506

Ravenstor Road
Wirksworth
Derbyshire DE4 4FY
0629 824848

East Region
Eastern Regional Office
Chancel House
East Street
Bingham
Nottinghamshire NG13 8DR
0949 37268

Wing D
Government Buildings
Prince of Wales Road
Dorchester
Dorset DT1 1QJ
0305 68558

1 The Crescent
Taunton
Somerset TA1 4EA
0823 276905

2nd floor
Highshore House
New Bridge Street
Truro
Cornwall TR1 2AA
0872 73531

South-East Region
South Eastern Regional Office
141 Castle Street
Salisbury
Wiltshire SP1 3TP
0722 336255

Agriculture House
55 Goldington Road
Bedford MK40 3LU
0234 61381

64a High Street
Braintree
Essex CM7 7JP
0376 47623

6–7 Town Lane
Newport
Isle of Wight P030 1JU
0983 528019

8 Romney Place
Maidstone
Kent ME15 6LE
0622 65222

Sussex House
212 High Street
Lewes
Sussex BN7 2NH
0273 471399

The Maltings
St John's Road
Wallingford
Oxfordshire OX10 9BZ
0491 35523

Barton Farm
Andover Road
Winchester
Hampshire SO22 6AX
0962 880503

The Crafts Council
Formed in 1971, the Crafts Council is appointed by the Minister for the Arts from whom it receives a grant to support the work of artist crafts people in England and Wales. In Scotland the work is done by the Scottish Development Agency. At present the Council has 22 members including practising crafts people and teachers. The Council can make grants for setting up workshops, employing a trainee, mounting exhibitions or advanced training. It can make loans to people who have been in business for at least two years in order to help them expand. For information about these and other activities contact the Crafts Council, 12 Waterloo Place, London SW1Y 4AU; 071–930 4811. In Scotland, contact the Scottish Development Agency, Small Businesses Division, Rosebery House, Haymarket Terrace, Edinburgh EH12 5EZ; 031–337 9595. (Government proposals currently under discussion suggest that the Crafts Council be merged with the much larger Arts Council.)

Local Development Boards
These are government agencies with responsibility for social and economic development in the areas they represent. They give advice, training, loans and grants and in some cases they provide starter factories on attractive terms to any enterprise which brings jobs to the area. The Boards are:

Enterprise Mid-Wales
Ladywell House
Newtown
Powys SY16 1JB
0686 26965

Local Enterprise Development Unit
Lamont House
Purdy's Lane
Newtownbreda
Belfast BT8 4TB
0232 691031

Highlands and Islands
Development Board
Bridge House
20 Bridge Street
Inverness IV1 1QR
0463 234171

Scottish Development Agency
Rosebery House
Haymarket Terrace
Edinburgh EH12 5EZ
031-337 9595

Welsh Development Agency
Small Business Unit
Treforest Industrial Estate
Pontypridd
Mid-Glamorgan CF37 5UT
044385 2666

The Training Agency

The Training Agency (previously briefly known as the Training Commission, and before that as the Manpower Services Commission) runs a series of programmes designed to prepare people for running their own businesses. Of these, the most extensive is the *Enterprise Allowance Scheme* which provides help during the first 12 months of self-employment. Anyone between 18 and 65, receiving unemployment benefit or Income Support, who has been out of work for at least eight weeks is eligible for the scheme provided that he or she has at least £1000 to invest in the business – from savings, a loan or overdraft. Participants are encouraged to seek free advice from the Small Firms Service and enterprise agencies. However, the main benefit of the scheme is that the applicant receives £40 a week for up to 52 weeks to supplement the receipts of the new business while it is being established. Since most new enterprises take some time to settle down, this is a very valuable bonus.

For further information on the Enterprise Allowance Scheme and the many other programmes run by the Training Agency, contact your local Job Centre or Department of Employment regional office (listed in the phone book) and ask for a copy of the booklet entitled 'Your Guide to our Employment, Training and Enterprise Programmes'.

Financial support

The government has, for some years, been promoting two schemes which are designed to help new or small businesses to expand. The first of these is the *Loan Guarantee Scheme*, designed to help new or small businesses to secure loans when they would have otherwise been unable to do so, either through lack of asset backing for the loan or through lack of a suitable track record. The loans are made by banks and the government guarantees a proportion of the loan – up to £75,000 or 70 per cent of the total, whichever is less. The borrower pays an extra 2½ per cent interest on the guaranteed proportion of the loan. First contact for a loan under this scheme is your bank manager.

The *Business Expansion Scheme* is designed to encourage wealthy individuals to make equity investments in small unquoted companies by allowing tax relief on such investments at top rates. If you wish to take advantage of such a scheme, either as business owner or investor your nearest Small Firms Centre (Freefone Enterprise) will send you some information.

Workshops

Managed workshops provide small units (from less than 100 square feet) usually in disused industrial premises which have been converted for occupation by dozens or scores of small businesses. The Saltaire Workshop in Bradford has converted a disused textile mill into 108 spaces, mostly in the 100–500 square feet range. Rents and periods of notice are kept as low as possible to encourage potential entrepreneurs to take the risk of starting or expanding a business in one of the units. A resident manager, sometimes with a small staff, looks after the letting and provides some common services.

A number of advanced industrial units, mostly factories and warehouses, have been built by development agencies in development areas. These are usually available for immediate occupation by tenants, sometimes with generous concessions on rents and rates in the early years. Although they are not specifically for small businesses, many of them would be suitable.

For information on any small workshop schemes, contact your local enterprise agency or Small Firms Service (Freefone Enterprise).

Tourist boards

Tourist boards in England, Scotland and Wales can give help, advice and financial support for tourism projects. These include hotel improvements, visitor attractions, leisure amenities, self-catering and tourism support services. If you have an idea and want to know whether it would qualify for assistance, you should contact one of the national or regional tourist boards. The addresses of the national boards are:

English Tourist Board
Thames Tower
Blacks Road
London W6 9EL
081–846 9000

Wales Tourist Board
Brunel House
2 Fitzallen Road
Cardiff CF2 1UY
0222 499909

Scottish Tourist Board
Croythorn House
23 Ravelston Terrace
Edinburgh EH4 3EU
031–332 2433

The Highlands and Islands
Development Board
Bridge House
20 Bridge Street
Inverness IV1 1QR
0463 234171

Nationalised industries

British Coal Enterprise (previously known as NCB Enterprise), BSC Industry and British Shipbuilders (Industry) have all been established by their respective nationalised industries to promote job creation in areas where unemployment has resulted from closures. Their main role is to provide support, normally in the form of loans, for people who wish to start new companies, expand existing ones, or relocate to one of the areas concerned. It must be emphasised that applicants do not need to be former employees of these organisations to qualify for such loans. For example, British Coal Enterprise will make loans normally up to five years for a maximum of 25 per cent of the total funding and at normal commercial rates, though lower initial rates or repayment holidays may also be part of the package. These bodies can help with the provision of sites, such as small workshops in redundant premises, and with training. They support enterprise agencies (see below) both by funding them and by staff secondments and they would frequently refer enquirers who need counselling to such agencies. British Rail have also shown their support for this activity by supporting the enterprise agencies in traditional railway areas such as Swindon.

In coal and steel closure areas, the European Coal and Steel Community (ECSC) provides 'soft loans' from £5000 to £4 million through agents such as banks and they provide loans direct for amounts exceeding £4 million. You may contact British Coal Enterprise and BSC Industry direct, through a bank or through an enterprise agency. The ECSC should be approached through a clearing bank or through Investors in Industry (3i) at 91 Waterloo Road, London SE1 8XP; 071–928 7822. The addresses of British Coal Enterprise and BSC Industry are:

British Coal Enterprise Ltd
14–15 Lower Grosvenor Place
London SW1W 0EX
071–630 5304

BSC Industry Ltd
Bridge House
Bridge Street
Sheffield S3 8NS
0742 731612

Banks

All the clearing banks are very active in attracting new small business clients and helping their existing clients to expand. As the small business sector has prospered during the 1980s the banks have discovered that making loans to such enterprises is a far easier and less troublesome way of earning a living than lending to South American governments. For this reason, they have all set up special departments which deal with small firms and which produce literature designed to attract small business customers – newsletters, start-up advice etc. Many of them have also set up regional offices which specialise in offering advice to small firms.

Business accounts are in general much more active than personal accounts and involve the branch in more work: paying in cheques and cash, producing statements etc. On the other hand, the small business's use of overdraft and loan facilities makes it very attractive to bank managers. I was very surprised, when I first opened a business account, to learn how much higher were my bank charges for my business account than for my personal account. I have never had complete success, despite persistent enquiries, in discovering just how banks assess bank charges on business accounts but I have the impression that branch managers enjoy a good deal of latitude in the matter. When opening a business account you should approach at least two banks since the experience of myself and other people starting businesses is that bank charges, interest rates etc, can vary significantly not only between the major clearing banks but between different branches of the same bank. Your first contact should be with your local branch manager and you should give him as much information as you can about such matters as:

Estimated sales
Cost of sales
Overheads
Profit
Cash flow
Loan and overdraft requirements
Weekly transactions, ie:
     Cheques and cash paid in
     Cheques and cash drawn out.

Ask each bank to tell you how they will calculate the bank charges as well as the level of interest on loan and overdraft. You may be surprised at the difference in cost between the cheapest and the most expensive bank. And remember that if your business is any good, the manager is just as anxious to have your account as you are to have his money! Your bargaining position is strong, so get the best deal you can.

Your local branch manager should be able to supply you with all the literature and other information made available to small business customers by the major banks but in case of difficulty you should contact the Small Firms Sections of the banks which are to be found at the following addresses:

Barclays Bank
Small Firms Division
Marketing Department
168 Fenchurch Street
London EC3P 3HP
071–283 8989

National Westminister Bank
Small Business Services
Third floor
8 Fenchurch Place
London EC3M 4PB
071–374 1000

Lloyds Bank
71 Lombard Street
London EC3P 3BS
071–260 8000

Midland Bank
Griffin House
41 Silver Street Head
Sheffield S1 3GG
0842 529232

Workers' co-operatives

There are about 500 workers' co-operatives in Britain. They should be distinguished from agricultural co-operatives (basically farmers who have formed groups to pool their buying or marketing power) and from consumers' co-operatives which are best known as the high street Co-op stores.

A workers' co-operative has three distinct characteristics. First, ownership and control are restricted to those who work for the organisation, though retired members are often allowed to retain their interest. There are thus no outside shareholders. Second, all permanent, full-time workers are members of the co-op. Third, the organisation is democratically controlled by the membership.

Workers' co-operatives originated in the mid-nineteenth century, mostly in craft industries, and their activities are still concentrated in labour-intensive businesses with retailing, printing, building services and crafts being well represented. In recent years they have sometimes been seen as a means of preserving or creating jobs. For example, in Scotland the Highlands and Islands Development Board promoted co-operatives in a number of fields including agriculture, fisheries and tourism with membership ranging from 50 to 500.

Most co-operatives, however, are small organisations with a dozen or so members and have often been helped to start by a grant or loan from a local authority wishing to promote employment. One such organisation emerged from a mothers and toddlers' group and was set on its way by a small loan from the local authority, providing office cleaning work on a part-time basis for about 20 people. Some co-operatives find that, when they reach a certain size, the co-operative form of organisation militates against effective management. Democratic control can lead to slow decision taking and threaten the future development of the organisation. In these circumstances the co-operative format may be abandoned in favour of a more conventional structure.

If you want to find out more about the possibility of starting a workers' co-operative in your area you can begin by contacting the Co-operative Development Agency at Broadmead House, 21 Panton Street, London SW1Y 4DR; 071–839 2988.

The Fullemploy Group

The Fullemploy Group was set up in 1979 with the principal aim of improving employment prospects for people from minority ethnic groups. It is mainly concerned with running training programmes for employment with the support of the Training Agency but it also runs enterprise courses for people who wish to start their own businesses. At present, ten Fullemploy Training Centres offer enterprise training courses and for details of these you should contact Fullemploy's head office at County House, 190 Great Dover Street, London SE1 4YB; 071–378 1774.

Head Start in Business

Head Start in Business is a training programme developed by the Industrial Society to prepare people for self-employment. The programme has been run in about 30 centres nationwide and is aimed particularly at long-term unemployed who need help in rebuilding confidence; ethnic minority groups and people born outside the UK with language difficulties; and people faced with redundancy who wish to establish whether self-employment is a viable future career option. The course consists of an introductory workshop which aims to give some insight into the world of self-employment and what it means to work for oneself. Of those attending the workshops about half go forward to the full training programme. If you wish to know more about courses which are being run in your area, please contact Vander Fitten Enterprise Unit, The Industrial Society, Peter Runge House, 3 Carlton House Terrace, London SW1Y 5DG; 071–839 4300.

Livewire

Livewire is an organisation designed to encourage young people to consider self-employment. It was established in 1982 and is heavily supported by the Shell UK Oil Company and locally by over 100 other private and public sector organisations. It is aimed particularly at people in the age group 16–25, of whom 4800 registered on the programme in 1988–89. Thirty per cent of these produced business plans for their own enterprises. Over 400 enterprises received an award in cash or in kind to help them develop their business.

For more information about the activities of Livewire in your area, please write to Livewire, 60 Grainger Street, Newcastle upon Tyne NE1 5JG; 091–261 5584.

Enterprise agencies

There are now over 300 enterprise agencies throughout the UK. It is difficult to generalise about them since each operates independently, funded mainly by the local community and actively promoted by the private sector funded organisation *Business In The Community*. A survey of 148 agencies estimated that about 40 per cent of their funding came from local authorities, 30 per cent from central government (via the Small Firms Service) and 30 per cent from industry and commerce. Banks, large local manufacturers and retailers are prominent among the financial supporters of enterprise agencies. Large companies also support the agencies by seconding staff to them on a full-time or part-time basis.

The constitution and precise objectives of each agency depend upon the local sponsors but the common aims of the agency network are, broadly, those of creating and preserving enterprises and jobs and helping small firms to expand. For example, the aims and objectives of the agency in Milton Keynes are:

1. To assist in the formation and ongoing management of commercially viable small businesses.
2. Through its various services, to help reduce the failure rate of existing small businesses.
3. To contribute towards employment.
4. To improve the local environment in which small businesses operate in Milton Keynes.

These aims may be taken as representative of those of other agencies.

In the present context, the main interest of the agencies lies in their role in helping to start new firms. A survey of seven provincial agencies in 1989 estimated that, between them, they had been involved in 2837 start-ups – an average of 405 start-ups per agency. A high proportion of the businesses started lay in the services sector which, as we have seen, is growing very rapidly. The agencies attributed the popularity of the services sector to the fact that such businesses require less capital in the start-up phase than most retail or manufacturing businesses. In many cases, people started up their businesses from home, thus reducing overheads and risk. The businesses started included catering, computing, car valet services, secretarial/bookkeeping, design and car phone fitting services. One of the most valuable services that the enterprise agency can offer is that of helping the would-be entrepreneur to think through the implications of his proposition and turn it into a viable business plan.

The managers of enterprise agencies are almost invariably people who have had many years of business experience. Sometimes they are men in their fifties and sixties who have been seconded to the agency by large companies who continue to pay their salaries until they reach the age of retirement. In other cases, they are run by young executives from banks whose employers want them to obtain front-line experience of business start-ups before taking a further step in their careers. In all cases, the experience, judgement and enthusiasm that these men can offer to a business starting up are of immense value. Moreover, they also have access to other sources of information. If you approach an agency with a proposal to set up a business in a field of which the agency manager has no experience, he can usually call upon the assistance of one of his many contacts among the agency's sponsors. All these services are free of charge.

In addition to counselling services of this kind, some agencies also run start-up courses, often sponsored by the Training Agency. Some of these are one-day 'start your own business' courses for people who are thinking of starting up, while the agency in Stevenage has enjoyed a lot of success running three-day small business courses for existing small entrepreneurs consisting of one day on finance, one on marketing and one on general management. Those agencies which do not run their own courses can normally put you in touch with other organisations such as local colleges which do run courses suited to your needs.

Enterprise agencies also act as the focus for other initiatives by local authorities combating unemployment. For example, they will be able to advise you of any special grants which apply to enterprises setting up in the area; and they will also know of any low-cost workshops and other units which may be suitable for an enterprise such as yours.

It is hard to emphasise too strongly the importance of contacting an enterprise agency before starting up a business or before taking any major steps to expand or diversify. The service is free so you have nothing to lose beyond the cost of a telephone call and a short trip to your local agency. On the other hand, the advice available there is invaluable. Surveys indicate that businesses which seek the assistance of an enterprise agency before starting up are three times more likely to survive the first year's trading than those which decide to go it alone without advice. What more can be said?

The names, addresses and telephone numbers of the agencies at present in operation are listed below by region.

North-East region

Alnwick
North Northumberland Enterprise
Agency
Hill House
39 Bondgate Within
Alnwick
Northumberland NE66 1SX
0665 605075

Ashington
SENET Enterprise Workshops
Green Lane
Ashington
Northumberland NE63 0EF
0670 811690

Barnard Castle
Teesdale Enterprise Agency
39 Galgate
Barnard Castle
County Durham DL12 8EJ
0833 31851

Bedlington Station
South East Northumberland Enterprise
Trust (SENET)
School Road
Bedlington
Northumberland NE22 7JB
0670 828686

Birtley
BEAM Ltd
Pinetree Centre
Durham Road
Birtley
Durham DH3 2TD
091-492 0022

Bishop Auckland
Wear Valley Enterprise Agency
St Helen Auckland Trading Estate
Bishop Auckland
County Durham DL14 9TX
0388 450505

Blyth
Plessey Road Workshops
Blyth
Northumberland NE24 4BN
0670 365558

Chester-le-Street
Chester-le-Street and City of Durham
Enterprise Agency (DCD)
Mechanics Institute
Newcastle Road
Chester-le-Street
County Durham DH3 3TS
091-389 2648

Consett
Derwentside Industrial Development
Agency
Berry Edge Road
Consett
County Durham DH8 5EV
0207 509124

Darlington
The Darlington and South West Durham
Business Venture Ltd
The Imperial Centre
Grange Road
Darlington
County Durham DL1 5PH
0325 480891

Durham City
32 Clay Path
Durham DH1 1QS
091-384 5407

Gateshead
Design Works (Gateshead) Ltd
William Street
Felling
Gateshead NE10 0JP
091-495 0066

Gateshead
1 Walker Terrace
Gateshead
Tyne & Wear NE8 1EB
091-477 6675

Hartlepool
Hartlepool Enterprise Agency Limited
Suite 7
Municipal Buildings
Church Square
Hartlepool
Cleveland TS24 7ER
0429 221216

Hartlepool New Development
Support Limited
Old Municipal Buildings
Upper Church Street
Hartlepool
Cleveland TS24 7ET
0429 867100

Hexham
Tynedale Business Centre
14 Gilesgate
Hexham NE46 3NJ
0434 603164

Middlesbrough
Cleveland Business Development
Agency Ltd
New Exchange Buildings
Queens Square
Middlesbrough TS2 1AA
0642 231389

Cleveland Youth Business Centres
6 North Street
Middlesbrough
Cleveland TS2 1JL
0642 240656

Morpeth
Northumberland Business Centre
Southgate
Morpeth
Northumberland NE61 2EH
0670 511221

Newcastle upon Tyne
The Tyne & Wear Enterprise Trust Ltd
(ENTRUST)
Portman House
Portland Road
Newcastle upon Tyne NE2 1BL
091-261 4838

Douglas House
Grainger Street
Newcastle upon Tyne NE1 5EW
091-261 9195

Newcastle Youth Enterprise Centre
25 Low Friar Street
Newcastle upon Tyne NE1 5UE
091-261 6009

St Thomas Street Workshops
St Thomas Street
Newcastle upon Tyne NE1 4LE
091-232 4895

Peterlee
East Durham Development Agency Ltd
5th floor
Lee House
Peterlee
Durham SR8 1BB
091-586 3366

Shildon
Shildon and Sedgefield District
Development Agency Ltd
BREL Offices
Byerley Road
Shildon
County Durham DL4 1PU
0388 777917

South Shields
The Tyneside Economic Development
Company Ltd (TEDCO)
Business Enterprise Centre
Eldon Street
South Shields
Tyne & Wear NE33 5JE
091-455 4300

Sunderland
Sunderland Youth Enterprise Centre
1–2 John Street
Sunderland
Tyne & Wear SR1 1UA
091-510 9191

Wallsend
81–83 High Street West
Wallsend
Tyne & Wear NE28 8JD
091-234 0895

North-West region

Accrington
Hyndburn Enterprise Trust
Eagle Street
Accrington
Lancashire BB5 1NS
0254 390000

Ashton-under-Lyne
Tameside Business Advice Service
Charlestown Industrial Estate
Turner Street
Ashton-under-Lyne OL5 8NS
061-339 8960

Barrow-in-Furness
Furness Business Initiative Ltd
Walney Road
Barrow-in-Furness
Cumbria LA14 5UG
0229 22132

Birkenhead
In Business Limited
The Business Centre
Claughton Road
Birkenhead
Wirral L41 6EY
051-647 7574

Cavendish Enterprise Centre Limited
Brassey Street
off Laird Street
Birkenhead
Wirral L41 8BY
051-653 4515

Blackburn
Blackburn and District Enterprise Trust
14 Richmond Terrace
Blackburn
Lancashire BB1 7BH
0254 664747 and 583862

Blackpool
Blackpool and Fylde Business
Agency Ltd
20 Queen Street
Blackpool
Lancashire FY1 1PD
0253 294929

Bolton
Bolton Business Ventures Limited
46 Lower Bridgeman Street
Bolton
Lancashire BL2 1DG
0204 391400

Bootle
South Sefton Enterprise Agency Ltd
Beaver Enterprise Workspace
58–60 Strand Road
Bootle
Merseyside L20 4BG
051-933 0024

Bury
Bury Enterprise Centre
Kay Street
Bury
Lancashire BL9 6BU
061-705 1878

Carlisle
Business Initiatives Carlisle
James Street
Carlisle
Cumbria CA2 5BB
0228 34120

Chester
Chester Enterprise Agency
Hoole Bridge
Chester CH2 3NQ
0244 311474

Cleator Moor
Enterprise West Cumbria
Cragg Road
Cleator Moor
Cumbria CA25 5PT
0946 813555

Clitheroe
Ribble Valley Enterprise Agency Ltd
Bank House
2 York Street
Clitheroe
Lancashire BB7 2DL
0200 22110

Crewe
SCOPE (South Cheshire Opportunity
for Private Enterprise)
SCOPE House
Weston Road
Crewe CW1 1DD
0270 58969

Congleton
Congleton Business Centre
Thomas Street
Congleton
CW12 1QU
0260 270022

Darwen
Blackburn and District Enterprise Trust
10 Borough Road
Darwen
Lancashire BB3 1PL
0254 72476

Ellesmere Port Neston
Entep Trust Ltd
72A Whitby Road
Ellesmere Port
South Wirral L65 0AA
051-356 3555

Fleetwood Garstang
Wyre Business Agency Ltd
WIBEC
19–21 Copse Road
Fleetwood
Lancashire FY7 6RP
0391 779279

Kendal
The Cumbria Rural Enterprise Agency
44–46 Lound Road
Kendal
Cumbria LA9 7DZ
0539 26624

Kirkby
Knowsley Enterprise Agency
Admin Building
Admin Road
Knowsley Industrial Park (North)
Kirby L33 7TX
051-548 3245

Lancaster
Business for Lancaster Ltd
32B St Leonard's House
St Leonardgate
Lancaster LA1 1NN
0524 66222

Leyland
South Ribble Business Venture Ltd
176 Towngate
Leyland
Lancashire PR5 1TE
0772 422242

Liverpool
Business in Liverpool Ltd
Merseyside Innovation Centre
131 Mount Pleasant
Liverpool L3 5TF
051-709 1231 and 1366

Merseyside Education Training
Enterprise Limited (METEL)
6 Salisbury Street
Liverpool L3 8DR
051-207 2281

Macclesfield
Macclesfield Business Ventures
Venture House
Cross Street
Macclesfield SK11 7PG
0625 615113

Manchester
Manchester Business Venture
c/o Manchester Chamber of
Commerce and Industry
56 Oxford Street
Manchester M60 7HJ
061-236 0153

Agency for Economic Development Ltd
8–12 Parisian Way
Moss Side Centre
Moss Lane East
Manchester M15 5NQ
061-226 9434

Maryport
Maryport Workspace
Solway Trading Estate
Maryport
Cumbria CA15 8NF
0900 815777

Northwich and Winsford
Vale Royal Small Firms Ltd
The Verdin Exchange
High Street
Winsford
Cheshire CW7 2AN
0606 861300

Oldham
Oldham Enterprise Agency
2 Prince Street
Rhodes Bank
Oldham 0L1 1EL
061-665 1225

Ormskirk
The West Lancashire Enterprise Trust
Limited
The Malt House
48 Southport Road
Ormskirk
Lancashire L39 1LX
06955 75488

Pendle
Pendle Enterprise Trust Ltd
19–23 Leeds Road
Nelson
Pendle
Lancashire BB9 9SZ
0282 698001

Penrith
The Cumbria Rural Enterprise Agency
Birbeck House
Duke Street
Penrith CA11 7NA
0768 68086

Preston
Preston Business Venture
Premier House
Church Street
Preston
Lancashire PR1 3BQ
0772 25723

Rawtenstall Bacup
Rossendale Enterprise Trust Ltd
29 Kay Street
Rawtenstall
Rossendale
Lancashire BB4 7LS
0706 229838

Rochdale
Metropolitan Enterprise Trust Rochdale
Area Ltd (Business Help)
Wellington Chambers
Smith Street
Rochdale 0L16 1TU
0706 356250

Runcorn
Business Link Limited
62 Church Street
Runcorn
Cheshire WA7 1LD
Tel: 0928 563037 and 573549

St Helens
The Community of St Helens Trust Ltd
PO Box 36
St Helens
Merseyside WA10 3TT
0744 696771

Sale
Trafford Business Venture
Third Floor
Six Acre House
Town Square
Sale
Cheshire M33 1XZ
061-905 2950

Salford
Salford Hundred Venture Ltd
Stamford House
361 Chapel Street
Salford
Manchester M3 5JY
061-835 1166

Skelmersdale
Business Development Unit
1 Westgate
Skelmersdale
Lancashire WN8 8LP
0695 29977

Southport
Southport Marketing and Enterprise
Bureau Ltd
Pavilion Buildings
99-105 Lord Street
Southport PR8 1RJ
0704 44173 and 43977

Stockport
Stockport Business Venture Limited
PO Box 66
Crossley Road
Heaton Chapel
Stockport SK4 5BH
061-432 3770

Warrington
Warrington Business Promotion Bureau
Barbauld House
Barbauld Street
Warrington WA1 2QY
0925 33309

Widnes
Business Link Limited
The Moor Lane Business Centre
Moor Lane
Widnes
Cheshire WA8 7AQ
051-423 6688

Wigan
Wigan New Enterprise Ltd
45 Bridgeman Terrace
Wigan
Lancashire WN1 1TT
0942 496591

Workington
Enterprise West Cumbria
Thirlmere Building
50 Lakes Road
Workington
Cumbria CA14 3YP
0900 65656

Yorkshire and Humberside Region

Barnsley
Barnsley Enterprise Centre
1 Pontefract Road
Barnsley S71 1AJ
0226 733291

Bradford
Bradford Enterprise Agency
Commerce House
Cheapside
Bradford
West Yorkshire BD1 4JZ
0274 734359

Castleford
Five Towns Resource and
Enterprise Centre
13–15 Sagar Street
Castleford WF10 1AG
0977 517191

Doncaster
DonBAC – The Doncaster Enterprise
Agency and Business Advice Centre
19–21 Hallgate
Doncaster DN1 3NA
0302 340320

Goldthorpe
Dearne Enterprise Centre
1 Barn Burgh Lane
Goldthorpe
Rotherham
South Yorkshire S63 9PG
0709 897703

Grimsby
The Grimsby and Cleethorpes Area
Enterprise Agency Ltd
10 Hainton Avenue
Grimsby
South Humberside DN32 9BB
0472 241869

Halifax
Calderdale Small Business Advice
Centre (CaSBAC)
OP 53
Dean Clough Office Park
Dean Clough
Halifax HX1 1XG
0422 369487

Huddersfield
Kirklees and Wakefield Venture Trust
Training Centre
Wakefield Road
Huddersfield HD1 5JP
0484 435523

Hull
Hull Business Advice Centre
24 Anlaby Road
Hull
North Humberside HU1 2PA
0482 27266

Leeds
Leeds Business Venture Ltd
Commerce House
2 St Alban's Place
Wade Lane
Leeds LS2 8HZ
0532 446474 and 457583

Richmond
Richmond and Northallerton Business
Venture Ltd
Enterprise House
Bridge Street
Bedale DL8 2AD
0677 23737

Rotherham
Rotherham Enterprise Agency Ltd
2nd Floor
All Saints Buildings
Corporation Street
Rotherham
South Yorkshire S60 1NX
0709 3821, Exts 3463 and 3464

Scarborough
Scarborough, Filey and District Business
Development Agency Ltd
The Sitwell Centre
Sitwell Street
Scarborough
North Yorkshire YO12 5EX
0793 354454

Sheffield
Sheffield Enterprise Agency (SENTA)
5 Palmerston Road
Sheffield
South Yorkshire SL10 2TE
0742 755721

Skipton
The Yorkshire Dales Enterprise Agency
Ltd (DEAL)
21 High Street
Gargrave
nr Skipton
North Yorkshire LS23 3RW
0756 748194

South Elmsall
Westfield Resource Centre
Westfield Lane
South Elmsall WF9 2PU
0977 45141

South Humber
South Humber Business Advice
Centre Ltd
7 Market Place
Brigg
South Humberside DN20 8HA
0652 57637

Treeton
Treeton Enterprise Centre
Rother Crescent
Treeton
Sheffield
South Yorkshire S60 5QY
0742 693033

Wath upon Dearne
Managed Workshops
Bolton Road
Wath upon Dearne
Rotherham
South Yorkshire S63 7JY
0709 879014

Whitby
Whitby and District Business
Development Agency Ltd
3 Bagdale
Whitby
North Yorkshire YO21 1QL
0947 600827

York
York Enterprise Ltd
York Enterprise Centre
1 Davygate
York YO1 2QE
0904 646803

The Vale of York Small Business
Association
Selby Enterprise Centre
23 Finkle Street
Selby YO8 0DT
0757 705567

West Midland Region

Birmingham
Birmingham Venture
Chamber of Commerce House
75 Harborne Road
Birmingham B15 3DH
021-454 6171

3B's Black Business in Birmingham
15 The Square
111 Broad Street
Birmingham B15 1AS
021-631 2860

Burton-on-Trent
Burton Enterprise Agency Ltd
Midland Railway Grain Warehouse
Derby Street
Burton-on-Trent DE14 2JJ
0283 37151

Cannock
Cannock and Burntwood Enterprise
Agency Ltd
80 High Street
Cannock
Staffordshire WS11 1BE
0543 71978

Coventry
Coventry Business Centre
Christchurch House
Greyfriars Lane
Coventry CV1 2GY
0203 552781

Dudley
Dudley Business Venture
Stanton House
10 Castle Street
Dudley
West Midlands DY1 1LQ
0384 231283

Hereford
The Herefordshire Enterprise
Agency Ltd
Berrows Business Centre
Bath Street
Hereford HR1 2HE
0432 276898

Lichfield
Lichfield Business Advisory Service
Redcourt House
Tamworth Street
Lichfield WS13 6PA
0543 258683

Nuneaton
Warwickshire Enterprise Agency
c/o The Ideas Centre
Vicarage Street
Nuneaton CV11 4BA
0203 345152

Redditch
Redditch Enterprise Agency Ltd
Rubicon Centre
17 Broad Ground Road
Lakeside
Redditch
Worcestershire B98 8YP
0527 501122

Solihull
Solihull Business Enterprise Ltd
Vulcan House
Vulcan Road
Lode Lane Industrial Estate
Solihull
West Midlands B91 9J1
021-704 1456

Stafford
Stafford Enterprise Limited
1–2 Eastgate Street
Stafford ST16 2NQ
0785 57057

Stoke on Trent
North Staffs and District
Business Initiative
Commerce House
Festival Park
Etruria
Stoke on Trent
Staffordshire ST1 5BE
0782 279013

Tamworth
Tamworth Business Advisory Service
Marmion House
Municipal Buildings
Lichfield Street
Tamworth B79 7BZ
0827 311222

Telford
Shropshire Enterprise Trust Ltd
Business Development Centre
Stafford Park 4
Telford
Shropshire TF3 3BA
0952 290782

Uttoxeter
East Staffs District Council
Uttoxeter Office
72 High Street
Uttoxeter
Staffordshire ST14 7JE
Tel: 0889 562341

Walsall
Walsall Small Firms Advice Unit Ltd
Jerome Chambers
Bridge Street
Walsall
West Midlands WS1 1EX
0922 646614

Warwick
Warwickshire Enterprise Agency
Northgate South
Northgate Street
Warwick CV34 4JH
0926 495685

West Bromwich
Sandwell Enterprise Ltd
Sandwell Business Advice Centre
Victoria Street
West Bromwich
Sandwell
West Midlands B70 8ET
021-569 2231 and 2562

Wolverhampton
Wolverhampton Enterprise Ltd
Exchange Street
Wolverhampton WV1 1TS
0902 312095

Worcester
Worcester Enterprise Agency
First Floor
Marmion House
Copenhagen Street
Worcester WR1 2HB
0905 612412

East Midlands Region

**Chesterfield, Claycross,
Dronfield, Eckington, Killmarsh**
North Derbyshire Enterprise Agency
123 Saltergate
Chesterfield
Derbyshire S40 1NH
0246 207379

Corby
Corby Industrial Development Centre
Grosvenor House
George Street
Corby
Northamptonshire NN17 1TZ
0536 62571

Derby
Derby and Derbyshire Business Venture
Saxon House
Heritage Way
Friary Street
Derby DE1 1NL
0332 360345

Grantham
South Lincolnshire Enterprise
Agency Ltd
Station Road
Grantham
Lincolnshire NG31 6HX
0476 68970

Kettering
Kettering Business Venture Trust Ltd
Douglas House
27 Station Road
Kettering
Northamptonshire NN15 7HH
0536 513840

Leicester
Leicester Business Venture Ltd
30 New Walk
Leicester
Leicestershire LE1 6TF
0533 554464

Lincoln
Lincoln Enterprise Agency
Innovation Centre
West Yard
Ropewalk
Lincoln LN6 7DQ
0522 40775

Mansfield
Mansfield Enterprise Partnership
The Old Town Hall
Market Place
Mansfield
Nottinghamshire NG18 1HX
0623 21773

Newark
Newark Enterprise Agency
The Firs
67 London Road
Newark
Nottinghamshire NG24 1RZ
0636 640666

Northampton
Northamptonshire Enterprise
Agency Ltd
Elgin House
Billing Road
Northampton NN1 5AU
0604 37401

Nottingham
Nottinghamshire Business Venture
City House
Maid Marian Way
Nottingham NG1 6BH
0602 470914

Ripley
Amber Valley Enterprise
3 Market Place
Ripley
Derbyshire
0773 570005

Eastern Region

Basildon
Basildon and District Local Enterpris
Agency Ltd
Keay House
88 Town Square
Basildon
Essex SS14 1BN
0268 286977

Braintree Witham and Halstead
Braintree District Enterprise Agency Ltd
Town Hall Centre
Market Square
Braintree
Essex CM7 6YG
0376 43140

Brentwood
Brentwood Enterprise Agency
1–2 Severn Arches Road
Brentwood
Essex CM14 4RG
0277 213405

Bury St Edmunds
Mid-Anglian Enterprise Agency Ltd
79 Whiting Street
Bury St Edmunds
Suffolk 1P33 1NX
0284 760206

Cambridge
Cambridge Enterprise Agency Ltd
71a Lensfield Road
Cambridge CB2 1EN
0223 323553

Chelmsford
Chelmsford Enterprise Agency Ltd
Unit A03
Globe House
New Street
Chelmsford
Essex CM1 1PP
0245 490281

Chelmsford, Basildon
Essex Business Centre
Chelmer Court
Church Street
Chelmsford
Essex CM1 1NH
0245 283030

Clacton-on-Sea, Harwich
Enterprise Tendring Ltd
27A Pier Avenue
Clacton-on-Sea
Essex CO15 1QE
0255 421225

Colchester
Colchester Business Enterprise Agency
154 Magdalen Street
Colchester
Essex CO1 2JT
0206 48833

Grays
Thurrock Local Enterprise Agency Ltd
79A High Street
Grays
Essex RM17 6NX
0375 374362

Great Yarmouth
Great Yarmouth Business Advisory
Service Ltd
Queens Road Business Centre
Queens Road
Great Yarmouth
Norfolk NR30 3HT
0493 850204

Harlow
Harlow Enterprise Agency Ltd
19 The Rows
The High
Harlow
Essex CM20 1DD
0279 38077

Hertford
Stort Valley Enterprise Trust
Wallfield Pegs Lane
Hertford SG13 8EQ
0279 55261

Huntingdon
Huntingdon Enterprise Agency Ltd
49 High Street
Huntingdon
Cambridgeshire PE18 6AQ
0480 450028

Ipswich
Ipsenta
18 Silent Street
Ipswich
Suffolk IP1 1TF
0473 259832

Kings Lynn
West Norfolk Enterprise Agency
Trust Ltd
41 Oldmeadow Road
Kings Lynn
Norfolk PE30 4JJ
0553 764127

Loughton
Forest Enterprise Agency Trust
Feat House
Rear of Swimming Pool
Traps Hill
Loughton
Essex 1G10 1SZ
081–508 7435

Lowestoft
Lowestoft Enterprise Trust Ltd
40 Gordon Road
Lowestoft
Suffolk NR32 1NL
0502 563286

Maldon
Maldon District Council
Planning Department
Princes Road
Maldon
Essex CM9 7DL
0621 54477

Norwich
Norwich Enterprise Agency Trust Ltd
112 Barrack Street
Norwich NR3 1TX
0603 613023

Peterborough
Peterborough Enterprise Programme
Broadway Court
Broadway
Peterborough
Cambridgeshire PE1 1RP
0733 310159

Southend
Southend Enterprise Agency Ltd
Commerce House
845 London Road
Westcliffe-on-Sea
Essex SS0 9SZ
0702 714115

Sudbury
Sudbury Enterprise Agency
Guthrie House
67 Cornard Road
Sudbury
Suffolk CO10 6XB
0787 73927

Wisbech
Fens Business Enterprise Trust Ltd
(FenBET)
27 Old Market
Wisbech
Cambridgeshire PE13 1NB
0945 587084

Southern Region

Aldershot
Blackwater Valley Enterprise Trust Ltd
The Old Town Hall
Grosvenor Road
Aldershot
Hampshire GU11 3DP
0252 319272

Alton, Petersfield, Bordon
East Hampshire Enterprise Ltd
c/o Bass Brewing (Alton) Ltd
Manor Park
Alton
Hampshire GU34 2PS
0420 87577

Andover
Basingstoke and Andover Enterprise
Centre
27–31 Bridge Street
Andover
Hampshire SP10 1BE
0264 332092

Ashford
Enterprise Ashford Ltd
Enterprise Centre
Old Railway Works
Newtown Road
Ashford
Kent TN24 0PD
0233 630307

Aylesbury
Aylesbury Vale Business Advice Scheme
23A Walton Street
Aylesbury
Buckinghamshire HP20 1TZ
0296 394555

Banbury
North Oxfordshire Business Venture
Ltd (NORBIS)
33a Crouch Street
Banbury
Oxfordshire OX16 9PR
0295 267900

Basingstoke
Basingstoke and Andover Enterprise
Centre
9 New Street
Joices Yard
Basingstoke
Hampshire RG21 1DF
0256 54041

Bedford
Bedfordshire Community Enterprise
Agency
Enterprise House
Old Ford End Road
Bedford MK40 4PH
0234 327422

Brighton
Brighton and Hove Business Enterprise
Agency Ltd
23 Old Steine
Brighton BN1 1EL
0273 688882

Camberley
Blackwater Valley Enterprise Trust Ltd
87 High Street
Camberley
Surrey GU15 3RN
0276 22226

Canterbury
East Kent Enterprise Agency
45 North Lane
Canterbury
Kent CT2 7EF
0227 470234

Chatham
Medway Enterprise Agency Ltd
Railway Street
Chatham
Kent ME4 4RR
0634 830301

Dartford
North West Kent Enterprise Agency
2A Hythe Street
Dartford
Kent DA1 1BT
0322 91451

Dorking
Surrey Business Enterprise Agency Ltd
c/o Bullimores
261 High Street
Dorking
Surrey RH4 1RL
0306 880880

Dover
East Kent Enterprise Agency
Western Road
Deal
Kent CT14 6PJ
0304 367673

Eastbourne
Eastbourne and District Enterprise
Agency Ltd
68 Grove Road
Eastbourne
East Sussex BN21 1DS
0323 644470

Folkestone, New Romney
Shepway Business Advisory Panel Ltd
24 Cheriton Gardens
Folkestone
Kent CT20 2AS
0303 59162

Gillingham
Medway Enterprise Agency Ltd
Marketing Centre
St George Centre
Chatham Maritime
Gillingham ME4 4UH
0634 44340

Gosport
Gosport Enterprise
Ferry Gardens
South Street
Gosport PO12 1EP
0705 586621

Gravesend
Gravesham Enterprise Agency
22 Wrotham Road
Gravesend
Kent DA11 0PA
0474 327118

Guildford
Surrey Business Enterprise Agency Ltd
28 Commercial Road
Guildford
Surrey GU1 4SU
0483 506969

Hastings
Hastings Business Ventures Ltd
18 Cornwallis Gardens
Hastings
East Sussex TN34 1LP
0424 433333

Hatfield
Welwyn and Hatfield Enterprise
Agency Ltd
5 Queensway House
Town Centre
Hatfield
Hertfordshire AL10 0NR
07072 67635

Hemel Hempstead
The Dacorum Enterprise Agency
Swallowdale Lane
Hemel Hempstead
Hertfordshire HP2 7EL
0442 232333

Isle of Wight
Isle of Wight Enterprise Agency Limited
6 Town Lane
Newport
Isle of Wight PO30 1JU
0983 529120

Lewes
Brighton and Hove Business Enterprise
Agency Ltd
Lewes House
High Street
Lewes BN7 2PC
0273 471600

Luton
Bedfordshire Community Enterprise
Agency (BECENTA)
Enterprise House
Gordon Street
Luton
Bedfordshire LU1 2QP
0582 452288

Maidstone
The Maidstone Enterprise Agency Ltd
5a Pudding Lane
Maidstone
Kent ME14 1PA
0622 675547

Milton Keynes
Milton Keynes Business Venture
Civic Offices (Level 3)
Saxon Gate East
Central Milton Keynes MK9 3JH
0908 660044

Newbury
Berkshire Enterprise Agency
Suite 2
The Old Town Hall
Newbury
Berkshire RG14 5ES
0734 523472

Oxford
Thames Business Advice Centre
8th Floor
Seacourt Tower
West Way
Oxford
Oxfordshire OX2 OJP
0865 249279

Portsmouth
Portsmouth Area Enterprise
27 Guildhall Walk
Portsmouth
Hampshire PO1 2RY
0705 833321

Reading
Berkshire Enterprise Agency
10–12 The Forbury
Reading
Berkshire RG1 3EJ
0734 585715

St Albans
St Albans Enterprise Agency Ltd
(STANTA)
Unit 6G
St Albans Enterprise Centre
Long Spring
Porters Wood
St Albans
Hertfordshire AL3 6EN
0727 37760

Sittingbourne
Swale Enterprise Agency
Crown Quay Lane
Sittingbourne
Kent ME10 3HP
0795 427623

**Southampton, Lyndhurst,
Eastleigh**
Southampton Enterprise Agency
Solent Business Centre
Millbrook Road West
Southampton
Hampshire SO1 OHW
0703 788088

Stevenage
Stevenage Initiative Ltd
Business and Technology Centre
Bessemer Drive
Stevenage
Hertfordshire SG1 2DX
0438 315733

Thanet
East Kent Enterprise Agency
Dane Valley Road
Broadstairs
Kent
0843 290205

Tonbridge
Great Weald Enterprise Agency
Peach Hall Depot
Tonbridge
Kent TN10 3HA
0732 360133

Watford
Watford Enterprise Agency
The Business Centre
Colne Way
Watford
Hertfordshire WD2 4ND
0923 247373

Woking
Surrey Business Enterprise Agency Ltd
19 High Street
Woking
Surrey GU21 1BW
0483 728434

Worthing
West Sussex Area Enterprise Centre Ltd
69a Chapel Road
Worthing
West Sussex
0903 31499

South-West Region

Barnstaple
North Devon Enterprise Agency Ltd
Yelland Centre
West Yelland
Barnstaple
Devon EX31 3EZ
0271 861215

Bath
Bath Enterprise Ltd
Green Park Station
Green Park Road
Bath BA1 1JB
0225 338383

Bradford on Avon
West Wiltshire Enterprise
PO Box 15
Abbey Mills
Bradford on Avon
Wiltshire BA15 1YZ
0221 67843

Bridgwater
Small Industries Group
68–70 Friarn Street
Bridgwater
Somerset TA6 3LJ
0278 424456

Bristol
Bristol and Avon Enterprise Agency
(BRAVE)
Bradford House
St Stephen's Avenue
Bristol BS1 1YL
0272 27222

Hartcliffe and Withywood Ventures L
HWV Block
Hartcliffe School
Bishport Avenue
Hartcliffe
Bristol BS13 0RL
0272 784865

New Work Trust Co Ltd
Avondale Workshops
Woodland Way
Kingswood
Bristol BS15 1QH
0272 603871

Bristol-St Paul's
The Coach House Small Business Centre
Upper York Street
St Paul's
Bristol BS2 8RH
0272 428022

Camborne
West Cornwall Enterprise Trust Ltd
Lloyds Bank Chambers
Market Square
Camborne
Cornwall TR14 8JT
0209 714914

Chippenham
North Wiltshire Enterprise Agency
Pearl Assurance Building
New Road
Chippenham
Wiltshire SN15 1EJ
0249 659275

Crediton
Mid Devon Enterprise Agency
Trevella Day Centre
Western Road
Crediton
Devon
0363 23145

Exeter
Business Enterprise Exeter
9 Marsh Green Road
Marsh Barton
Exeter EX2 8PN
0392 56060

Falmouth
West Cornwall Enterprise Trust Ltd
7 Church Street
Falmouth
Cornwall TR11 3DS
0326 311690

Frome
Frome and Mendip Enterprise Agency
South Parade
Frome
Somerset BA11 1EJ
0373 73101

Glastonbury
Face Enterprise Agency
17–18 Market Place
Glastonbury
Somerset BA6 9HL
0458 33917

Gloucester
Gloucestershire Enterprise Agency
19–21 Brunswick Road
Gloucester GL1 1HG
0452 501411

Honiton
East Devon Small Industries Group
115 Border Road
Heath Park
Honiton
Devon EX14 8BT
0404 41806

Jersey
Jersey Business Venture
15 Broad Street
St Helier
Jersey
Channel Islands
0534 35168

Kingsbridge
Tindle Enterprise Centre
101–103 Fore Street
Kingsbridge
Devon TQ7 1AF
0548 6850

Launceston
Enterprise Tamar
National School
St Thomas Road
Launceston
Cornwall PL15 8BU
0566 5632

Liskeard
Caradon Business Centre
Station Road
Liskeard
Cornwall
0759 44433

Newton Abbot
Teignbridge Enterprise Agency
The Tindle Centre
St Marychurch Road
Newton Abbot
Devon TQ12 4UQ
0626 67534

Paulton
Wansdyke Enterprise Agency
Business Advice Centre
High Street
Paulton
Bristol BS18 5NW
0761 415400

Penzance
West Cornwall Enterprise Trust Ltd
Buriton House
Alverton
Penzance
Cornwall TR18 2QP
0736 67508

Plymouth
Enterprise Plymouth Ltd
Somerset Place
Stoke
Plymouth PL3 4BB
0752 569211

Poole, Weymouth, Isle of Purbeck
Dorset Enterprise Agency Ltd
1 Britannia Road
Lower Parkstone
Poole
Dorset BH14 8AZ
0202 748333

St Austell
Restormel Local Enterprise Trust Ltd
Lower Penarwyn
St Blazey
Park
Cornwall PL24 2DS
0726 813079

Salisbury
South Wiltshire Enterprise Agency
52 Endless Street
Salisbury
Wiltshire SP1 2PH
0722 411052

Shepton Mallet
Frome and Mendip Enterprise Agency
27 Brewmaster Buildings
Charlton Industrial Estate
Shepton Mallet
Somerset BA4 5QE
0749 342817

Swindon
Great Western Enterprise
Emlyn Square
Swindon
Wiltshire SN1 5BP
0793 488088

Taunton
Small Industries Group
23 High Street
Taunton
Somerset TA1 3PJ
0823 336600

Tavistock
West Devon District Council Offices
Kilworthy Park
Tavistock
Devon
0752 569211

Tiverton
Mid Devon Enterprise Agency
The Factory
Leat Street
Tiverton
Devon EX16 5LL
0884 255629

Totnes
Dart Business Centre
Skinners Bridge
Dartington
Totnes
Devon TQ9 6JE
0803 862271

Warmley
New Work Trust Co Ltd
Marketing Centre
London Road
Warmley
Bristol BS15 5JH
0272 601109 and 677807

Weston-Super-Mare
Woodspring Enterprise Agency
Elizabeth House
30–32 The Boulevard
Weston-Super-Mare
Avon BS23 1NF
0934 418118

Yate
North Avon Business Centre
Dean Road
Yate
Bristol BS17 5NH
0454 317888

Yeovil
The Enterprise Agency (South Somerset
and West Dorset)
5 St Johns House
Church Path
Yeovil
Somerset BA2 0HF
0935 79813

London Region

Barking
The North East Thames Business
Advisory Centre
Abbey Hall
Axe Street
Barking
Essex 1G11 7LZ
0708 766438

Brentford
Enterprise Hounslow Ltd
13 Boston Manor Road
Brentford TW8 9DT
081–847 3269

Brixton
South London Business Initiative Ltd
444 Brixton Road
Suite 113–114
Brixton Enterprise Centre
London SW9 8EJ
071–274 4000, Ext 375

Bromley
Bromley Enterprise Agency Trust Ltd
7 Palace Grove
Bromley
Kent BR1 3HA
081–290 6568

Camden Town
Camden Enterprise Ltd
57 Pratt Street
Camden
London NW1 0DP
071–482 2128

Cricklewood
Brent Business Venture Ltd
177 Cricklewood Broadway
London NW2 2HT
081–450 6270

Croydon
Croydon Business Venture Ltd
74 Cherry Orchard Road
Croydon
Surrey CR0 6BA
081–681 8339 and 8330

Deptford
Deptford Enterprise Agency
146 Deptford High Street
Deptford
London SE8 3PQ
081–692 9204

Ealing
Enterprise Ealing Ltd
69–71 Broadway
West Ealing
London W13 3PT
081–840 2667

Edmonton, Ponders End
Enfield Enterprise Agency
2–3 Knights Chambers
32 South Mall
Edmonton Green
London N9 0TL
081–807 5333

Finchley
Barnet Enterprise Trust Limited (Barnet)
Hertford Lodge
East End Road
Finchley
London N3 3QE
081–346 2187

Finsbury Park
North London Business
Development Agency
35–37 Blackstock Road
Finsbury Park
London N4 2JF
071–359 7405

Hackney
Hackney Business Venture
277 Mare Street
London E8 1EB
081–533 4599

Harrow
The Harrow Enterprise Agency Ltd
2 Courtfield Avenue
Harrow
Middlesex HA1 2LW
081–427 6188

Ilford
The North East Thames Business
Advisory Centre
Broadway Chambers
1 Cranbrook Road
Ilford
Essex 1G1 4DU
081–553 4029

Islington
Manor Gardens Enterprise Centre
10–18 Manor Gardens
London N7 6JY
071–272 8944

London
London Enterprise Agency (LEntA)
4 Snow Hill
London EC1A 2BS
071–236 3000

Morden
Merton Enterprise Agency Ltd
12th Floor
Crown House
London Road
Morden
Surrey SM4 5DX
081–545 3067

Paddington
Westminster Enterprise Agency Ltd
9 Praed Street
London W2 1NS
071–706 4260

Romford
The North East Thames Business
Advisory Centre
Marshalls Chambers
30A South Street
Romford
Essex RM1 1RP
0708 766438

Ruislip
Hillingdon Enterprise Agency Ltd
100a Long Lane
Hillingdon
Middlesex UB10 9PG
0895 73433

Sutton
Sutton Enterprise Agency Ltd
11 Lower Road
Sutton
Surrey SM1 4QJ
081–643 9430

Tower Hamlets
Tower Hamlets Centre for Small
Business Ltd
76 Wentworth Street
London E1 7SE
071–377 8821

Twickenham
Richmond upon Thames Enterprise
Agency Ltd
55 Heath Road
Twickenham
Middlesex TW1 4AW
081–891 3742

Wales

Aberdare
The Business Centre
The Gadlys Centre
Aberdare
Mid-Glamorgan CF44 8DL
0685 882515

Amman Valley
Dinefwr Enterprise Company
Towey Valley Business Centre
Talley Road
Llandeilo
Dyfed SA19 7HR
0558 823863

Bargoed
Economic Development Partnership of
the Rhymney Valley
Enterprise Centre
Bowen Industrial Estate
Aberbargoed
Bargoed
Mid-Glamorgan CF8 9EP
0443 821222

Barry
Barry Business Advice Centre
55A Holton Road
Barry
South Glamorgan CF6 6HF
0446 721361

Bridgend
Ogwr Partnership Trust Ltd
Enterprise Centre
Bryn Road
Tondu
Bridgend
Mid-Glamorgan CF32 9BS
0656 724414

Cardiff
Cardiff and Vale Enterprise
Enterprise House
127 Bute Street
Cardiff CF1 5LE
0222 494411

Deeside
Deeside Enterprise Trust Ltd
Park House
Deeside Industrial Park
Deeside
Clwyd CH5 2NZ
0244 815262

Haverfordwest
Pembrokeshire Business Initiative (PBI)
Lombard Chambers
14 High Street
Haverfordwest
Dyfed SA61 2LD
0437 767655

Holywell
Delyn Business Partnership Ltd
Greenfield Business Park
Bagillt Road
Holywell
Clwyd CH8 7HN
0352 711747

Llandrindod Wells
Powys Self Help
Old Town Hall
Temple Street
Llandrindod Wells
Powys LD1 5DL
0597 4576

Llanelli
Llanelli Enterprise Company Ltd
100 Trostre Road
Llanelli
Dyfed SA15 2EA
0554 772122

Merthyr Tydfil
Merthyr-Aberdare Development
Enterprise Ltd
The Enterprise Centre
Merthyr Industrial Park
Pentrebach
Merthyr Tydfil
Mid-Glamorgan CF48 4DR
0443 692233

Neath
Neath Development Partnership
Enterprise Ltd
7 Water Street
Neath SA11 3EP
0639 634111

Newport
Newport Enterprise Agency Ltd
Enterprise Way
off Bolt Street
Newport
Gwent NP9 2AQ
0633 254041

Ruthin, Chirk
Clwydfro Enterprise Agency
Llysfasi
Ruthin
Clwyd LL15 2LB
0978 88414

Swansea, Pontardulais
West Glamorgan Enterprise Trust Ltd
12A St Mary's Square
Swansea
West Glamorgan SA1 3LP
0792 475345

Northern Ireland

Armagh
Armagh Business Centre
2 Loughgall Road
Armagh BT61 7NH
0861 525050

Bangor
North Down Development
Organisation
Enterprise House
Balloo Industrial Estate
Bangor
County Down BT19 2QT
0247 271525

Belfast
Action Resource Centre
103 York Street
Belfast BT15 1AB
0232 328000

Brookfield Business Centre Ltd
Brookfield Mill
333 Crumlin Road
Belfast BT14 7EA
0232 745241

Carrickfergus
Carrickfergus Enterprise Ltd
Kilroot Park
Larne Road
Carrickfergus
County Antrim BT38 7PR
0960 351095

Coleraine
Coleraine Enterprise Agency
Louganhill Industrial Estate
Coleraine
County Londonderry BT52 2NR
0265 56318

Downpatrick
Jobspace (NI) Ltd
45 Saul Road
Downpatrick
County Down BT30 6PA
0396 616416

Draperstown
Workspace Draperstown Ltd
7 Tobermore Road
Draperstown
Magherafelt BT45 7AG
0648 28113

Dunmurry
Glenwood Enterprises Ltd
Springbank Industrial Estate
Pembroke Loop Road
Dunmurry BT17 0QL
0232 610311

Enniskillen
Fermanagh Enterprise Ltd
Cross Street
Enniskillen
County Fermanagh BT74 7BD
0365 23117

Larne
Larne Enterprise Development
Company
Ledcom Industrial Estate
Bank Road
Larne
County Antrim BT40 3AW
0574 70742

Londonderry
Ebrington Business Centre Ltd
Ebrington Gardens
Waterside
Londonderry BT47 1EH
0504 43885

Newry
Newry and Mourne Enterprise Agency
Enterprise House
5 Downshire Place
Newry BT34 1DZ
0693 67011

Omagh
Omagh Enterprise Company Ltd
Gortrush Industrial Estate
Derry Road
Omagh
County Tyrone BT78 5EJ
0662 49494

Portadown
Craigavon Industrial Development
Organisation
Craigavon Enterprise Centre
Carn Industrial Estate
Portadown BT63 5RH
0762 333393

Scotland

Aberdeen
Aberdeen Enterprise Trust
First Floor
Seaforth Centre
30 Waterloo Quay
Aberdeen AB2 1BS
0224 582599

Alloa
Alloa and Clackmannan Enterprise
Trust (ACE)
Whins Road
Alloa
Clackmannanshire FK10 3SA
0259 72154

Arbroath
Arbroath Venture Trust
115 High Street
Arbroath DD11 1DP
0241 70563

Ayr
Ayr Locality Enterprise Resource Trust
Ltd (ALERT)
88 Green Street
Ayr KA8 8BG
0292 264181

Coatbridge
Monklands Business Enterprise Trust
Unit 10
Coatbridge Business Centre
Main Street
Coatbridge ML5 3RB
0236 23281

**Crossgates, Dunfermline,
Kirkcaldy**
South Fife Enterprise Trust Ltd
6 Main Street
Crossgates
Fife KY4 8AJ
0383 515053

Cumbernauld
Cumbernauld and Kilsyth Enterprise
Trust Ltd
5 South Muirhead Road
Cumbernauld G67 1AJ
0236 739394

Cumnock
Cumnock and Doon Enterprise Trust
Cumnock and Doon Enterprise Centre
Block 3
Caponacre Industrial Estate
Cumnock
Ayrshire KA18 1LD
0290 21159 and 25303

Dalkeith
Midlothian Campaign
115 High Street
Dalkeith
Midlothian EH22 1AX
031–660 5849

Dumbarton
Dumbarton District Enterprise Trust
Block 2/2
Vale of Leven Industrial Estate
Dumbarton
Dunbartonshire G82 3PD
0389 50005 and 55424

Dumfries, Annan, Castle Douglas, Sanquhar
The Enterprise Trust for Nithsdale, Annandale/Eskdale and the Stewartry
Heathhall
Dumfries DG1 1TZ
0387 56229

Dundee
Dundee Enterprise Trust Ltd
West Hendersons Wynd
Dundee DD1 5BY
0382 26002

East Kilbride
East Kilbride Business Centre
PO Box 1
10th Floor
Plaza Tower
East Kilbride G74 1NW
0355 238456

Edinburgh
Edinburgh Venture Enterprise Trust
(EVENT)
30 Rutland Square
Edinburgh EH1 2BW
031–229 8928

Leith Enterprise Trust
25 Maritime Street
Leith
Edinburgh EH6 5PW
031–553 5566

Edinburgh Old Town Trust
Advocate's Close
High Street
Edinburgh EH1 1PS
031–225 8818

Elgin
Moray Enterprise Trust
6 North Guildry Street
Elgin 1V30 1JR
0343 548391

Falkirk
Falkirk Enterprise Action Trust (FEAT)
New House Road
Grangemouth FK3 8LL
0324 665500

Fraserburgh
Fraserburgh Ltd
Old Station Yard
Dalrymple Street
Fraserburgh AB4 5BH
0346 27764

Glasgow
Glasgow Opportunities
7 West George Street
Glasgow G2 1EQ
041–221 0955

The Greater Easterhouse Partnership
40 Township Centre
Easterhouse
Glasgow G34 9DT
041–771 5591

Barras Enterprise Trust
244 Gallowgate
Glasgow G4 0TS
041–552 7258

Glenrothes
Glenrothes Enterprise Trust Ltd
312 North Street
Glenrothes
Fife KY7 5PV
0592 757903 and 759584

Greenock
Inverclyde Enterprise Trust Ltd
64–66 West Blackhall Street
Greenock PA15 1XG
0475 892191

Hamilton
Life
116 Cadzow Street
Hamilton
Lanarkshire ML3 6HP
0698 891515

Inverness
Highland Opportunity Ltd
Development Department
Highland Regional Council
Glenurquhart Road
Inverness 1V3 5NX
0463 234121, Ext 402

Kilbirnie
Garnock Valley Development
Executive Ltd
44 Main Street
Kilbirnie
Ayrshire KA25 7BY
0505 685455

Kilmarnock
The Kilmarnock Venture
Enterprise Trust
30 The Foregate
Kilmarnock KA1 1JH
0563 44602

Kirkintilloch
Strathkelvin Enterprise Trust
10 Rochdale Place
Kirkintilloch G66 1HZ
041–777 7171

Leven
Levenmouth Enterprise Trust
Unit 17b–20a
Hawkslaw Trading Estate
Riverside Road
Leven
Fife KY8 4LT
0333 27905

Motherwell
Motherwell Enterprise Trust
28 Brandon Parade
Motherwell ML1 1UJ
0698 69333

Newton Stewart
Wigtown Rural Development
Company Ltd
Royal Bank Building
44 Victoria Street
Newton Stewart
Wigtownshire DG8 6BT
0671 3434

Paisley
Paisley and Renfrew Enterprise Trust
27a Blackhall Street
Paisley PA1 1TD
041–889 0010

Pitlochry
Highland Perthshire Development
Company Ltd
21 Bonnethill Road
Pitlochry
Perthshire PH16 5BS
0796 2697

Saltcoats
Ardrossan, Saltcoats and Stevenston
Enterprise Trust (ASSET)
Estate Office
The APL Centre
Stevenston Industrial Estate
Stevenston
Ayrshire KA20 3LR
0294 605121

Stirling
Stirling Enterprise Park
John Player Building
Stirling FK7 7RP
0786 63416

CHAPTER 10

Ideas in Action

The first part of this chapter features eight case studies of people who have started their own successful businesses, often in the most unpromising circumstances. The people concerned cover a very wide range of ages, education and experience. The only thing that they have in common is that they are all successful entrepreneurs. It is not suggested that you should necessarily follow any of them into the markets in which they have succeeded, though in some cases there are clearly opportunities for others to do so. However, I hope that their examples will stimulate others to show the same spirit of enterprise. The second part briefly describes a number of more familiar business opportunities, some of them, like networking and mail order, being very heavily promoted. I have tried to suggest ways in which you can decide whether these are right for you.

Jim Butcher and Colin Hill – Pottery Portraits

I first met Jim Butcher in the summer of 1987. I was writing a book about people who run businesses from home and I had learned about Jim's business in the course of my research for the book. He had taken early retirement through disability and started to look for a business opportunity which would enable him to supplement his pension. Before retiring, Jim worked for 20 years as a ticket inspector which made him, in his own words 'a suspicious blighter', so when he saw an advertisement for a machine that promised to provide a steady income for a few hours' work each week he thought it sounded too good to be true. He decided to investigate. He travelled from his home on the outskirts of London to Anglesey, off the coast of North Wales, where the machine is made. He checked it out, bought the machine and was soon earning a steady £500 for a few hours' work each week.

The product he sells is a *Pottery Portrait*, a unique, distinctive and personalised memento. It consists of a photograph (colour or black and white) which is glazed permanently on to a plate using a simple technique which can be learned in half an hour. The market is impossible to measure simply because it's so new. Only in the last few years has the service started to become available in some parts of the UK and in most areas it is still virtually unknown. Nearly everyone has photographs of children, pets, family occasions, weddings, holidays etc, which they either frame or stick in albums. This technique enables them to turn some of these photographs into unique and permanent mementos which will be a source of pride and pleasure and there is plenty of repeat business to be had from satisfied customers. Mothers who order a portrait of a young child will return with more orders as their families grow in size and number – the first day at school, the football match, the skiing holiday, the graduation, the wedding and so on. Further ideas for developing the business are given below.

There are several glazing machines on the market, widely advertised, but the one used by Jim Butcher and recommended by him for its combination of performance, reliability and cost, is made in Britain by Pottery Portraits Ltd, Heulfre, Caergeiliog, Isle of Anglesey; telephone 0407 742020. There are two machines in the Pottery Portraits range, varying in the number of plates they can glaze at a time. The smaller one, about the size of a large typewriter, will glaze three 6-inch diameter plates at a time and costs £475 plus VAT. The larger machine will glaze 12 6-inch diameter plates at a time and costs £660 plus VAT. Both machines take larger plates though in smaller numbers. In addition, a starter kit containing knives, templates, circle cutter, glaze etc, costs a further £75.50 plus VAT. You will also need a supply of plates which you can buy from anywhere. If you buy them from Pottery Portraits a kit of about 80–100 plates plus hangers and display stands will cost about £150.

The glazing process is very easy to understand. First, you cut the photograph to the required size for the plate which has been chosen, using the equipment supplied with the machine starter kit. You fix the photograph to the plate with adhesive tape and then apply a thin coat of glaze to the surface of the photograph. You put the plate in the machine and switch it on. After four minutes the machine automatically switches itself off and your plate now has the picture permanently bonded to it to give a product which is literally unique. The plates, once photographs have been glazed on to them, are for ornamental use only.

Profit margins on the plates are substantial. A 6-inch round plate, which is one of the most popular items, can be purchased at wholesale prices for less than £1 and when glazed, Jim sells it for £6. The cost of glaze, adhesive tape and electricity vary from 35p to 65p per item depending upon the amount of glaze you use and the size of the plate.

Jim markets his service through 12 local agents – hairdressers, photographers, florists, pet shops and playgroups, all within easy walking distance of his home. He leaves a sample plate with each agent as an advertisement for his service. The agent receives 20 per cent commission on sales. Jim visits each agent twice a week, collecting new orders and delivering completed ones.

I also interviewed Colin Hill who lives in the North of England and operates in a different way from Jim Butcher. In November 1986, Colin, who had been made redundant, borrowed £900 from a friend and bought a starter kit plus plates. Within six months he had paid back the loan, plus £150 interest and bought a car with the profits of the business. Colin doesn't use agents at all. He knocks on doors, shows a sample of his works and takes orders. His weekly profit averages £250–£300 and rarely drops below £200 even at quiet times of the year. On the back of each plate, Colin sticks a self-adhesive label with his telephone number and this produces a lot of repeat business. He does particularly well on the council estate not far from his home and he never asks for a deposit when taking an order. This instils confidence in his customers and he has hardly ever had a bad debt.

This is a market which is still comparatively new and appears to have a lot of potential though you must, of course, undertake research in your own area to satisfy yourself that there is a real opportunity. Here are some ideas which you might like to pursue when making your own enquiries. They are based on the experience of Jim and Colin in their businesses.

> *Playgroups, nurseries and schools.* Parents like to have distinctive portraits of their children at different stages of their development; schools like to raise money. Approach some of your local establishments offering to make the service available in return for donating a share of the payment to fund-raising activities.
>
> *Fêtes, exhibitions, pet shows etc.* An excellent source of publicity as well as on-the-spot business if you can take photographs.
>
> *Sports clubs.* Teams from schools, local amateur clubs etc, may appreciate a permanent memorial of a successful season; also anniversaries and big matches. The same applies to local drama and operatic societies.
>
> *Limited editions.* Produce your own designs or commemorate local events or buildings; eg portraits of your local church or town hall in association with their own fundraising.
>
> *Business gifts.* Many businesses give diaries, calendars etc to their customers which are immediately thrown away. A distinctive gift could be produced by this method such as a paperweight or desk organiser incorporating the name and address of the donor plus photographs of his products.

The import/export agents

Tom Issa

I regularly see advertisements and receive mail shots telling me how easy it is to set up an import/export business and make a great deal of money in the process. Like all schemes which promise a great deal of money for not too much work, these should be treated with caution, but Tom Issa is evidence of the fact that it is possible to run a successful import/export business provided that you approach it in the right way and learn from your experience.

Tom completed his 'A' levels in 1983 and then undertook a four-year honours degree course in European Business Studies at the Buckinghamshire College. One of the features of the course was that he spent a year studying and working in Germany where he learned to speak German fluently. He was also required, under the supervision of an experienced tutor, to complete a dissertation on a business topic and he decided to write his on the potential market in West Germany for small electrical appliances made in Great Britain. Having written the dissertation, he was convinced that there were many opportunities to be exploited in the West German market of which British manufacturers were unaware.

On completing his degree, therefore, he immediately set up a limited company called Issa Europe Ltd, which was designed to seek out and exploit these opportunities. He approached a number of major British manufacturers and offered to seek out opportunities for them through the contacts he had made in Germany while writing his dissertation. A major British manufacturer made use of his services in securing official German approval from the German Standards Board (known as TVG) and this enabled them to start selling in Germany.

Tom also made some mistakes in his early days which have strongly influenced the way he operates. For example, he spent a great deal of time setting up contacts for a foreign gentleman who kept promising him major government contracts which eventually came to nothing. Another major manufacturer, having benefited from Tom's expertise in setting up a contact with a German wholesaler, proceeded then to cut him out of the operation and deal directly with the wholesalers themselves.

As a result of these experiences, Tom now always charges a consultancy fee when seeking out contacts and his normal practice is to act as a merchant rather than an agent. This is an important distinction. An agent puts a supplier in contact with a customer and takes a commission on the resulting sales but he is vulnerable if an unscrupulous supplier decides to deal direct with the customer. A merchant purchases items on his own account from a supplier and then sells them on to the customer, taking a mark-up in the process. Thus the supplier and customer do not come into direct contact with each other. There is, of course, always the risk that a merchant will be left with merchandise which he has purchased but which the customer does not want to take from him. However, Tom has managed to avoid this since he always secures the order from the customer before he commits himself to the supplier.

Most of his contacts are made through exhibitions and through advertisements which he takes in *Kellys Directory* and *Export Times*. He finds that many English companies are surprisingly unenthusiastic about export opportunities but speaks very highly of the Scots. As he showed me, one small Scottish company called Walkers of Aberlour-on-Spey do everything right! They have multilingual descriptions on their packs, they respond promptly to requests for information and prices and their record in despatching orders on time is exemplary. Consequently, Tom is able to send large quantities of their high quality gift food packs to German mail order companies.

Tom at present specialises in gift foods, knitwear (which he also exports to France) and electrical goods. While setting up a deal for the sale of trouser presses in Germany his attention was drawn to a German machine for cleaning shoes, suitable for installation in hotels. Sensing an opportunity, he made some enquiries in Great Britain and discovered that the range of UK products available was very limited. He therefore contacted the purchasing departments of the 50 largest hotel groups (by telephone), followed this up with a mail shot to 5000 hotels, and is now supplying these machines to a number of leading hotel groups.

Tom speaks very highly of the Department of Trade and Industry as a source of information on UK suppliers. He finds that their response to his requests for lists of suppliers of a very wide variety of products is always prompt and efficient. He has also found invaluable a book called *Croner's A-Z of Business Information Sources* which he bought from Croner Publications of Kingston upon Thames, Surrey. As he approaches the end of his second year of trading, Tom's annual sales are well on the way to a half a million pounds and he plans to raise this to £1 million per annum within two to three years. He has done all this with one German-speaking assistant.

I asked him what he believes to be the most valuable lessons he has learned in the last two years. His reply to this was revealing: 'I've never lost an order: orders get treated with kid gloves.' This means that he sometimes has to spend time chasing up his suppliers in order to ensure that his customers obtain the products they want, when they want them, but it means that he has also built up a reputation as a reliable supplier to whom his customers turn first when they need something. The second thing he has learned is always to be alert to opportunities. These can be picked up at fairs and exhibitions or from casual conversations, as when he learned of the opportunity for importing shoe cleaning equipment from one of his German contacts.

Tom's business owes its origins to a piece of academic work which he was obliged to do in order to obtain a degree. Upon the few contacts that he then established he has built a substantial and rapidly growing business which he plans to take into new products, new markets and new countries in the next few years. I have no doubt that he will succeed.

Michael LeFroy

It is interesting to compare Tom's experience with that of Michael LeFroy who developed a successful import/export business on an entirely different basis. Michael was the export sales manager of a large company in the fire prevention business. During the course of his work he met a customer, based in Scandinavia, who sold a range of electrical controls which could be used as a component in many kinds of equipment – for example, fire prevention, telephone systems and battery chargers.

Michael is not a trained engineer but he has the salesman's ability to spot an opportunity and he knew from his contacts in the industry that there was a need among many UK manufacturers for components of the kind the Scandinavian company could supply. He spent the next 18 months, working in the evenings and at weekends, estimating the potential demand for the product he had seen, while continuing to work as an export sales manager in order to provide his young family with a secure income.

Once he had become convinced that there really was a demand for the product, he set up a joint venture operation with the Scandinavians and proceeded to import the products and distribute them in the UK market. Since he had limited capital and had to keep his overheads down, his centre of operations became his spare bedroom. He appointed an import agent to handle administration and to deliver goods to the customers so that he could concentrate on the task for which he was best prepared – selling the products. Since most of his potential customers were very large organisations like GEC, the Electricity Boards and British Gas, Michael thought it best to conceal the fact that his was such a small operation. He installed a separate business telephone line, acquired a PO Box No as his address, printed some high quality business stationery and arranged to give presentations on the premises of his clients or, when necessary, in hotels.

Within 18 months sales had reached £200,000, at which point he moved out of the spare bedroom and rented 800 square feet of storage space on a nearby trading estate. A year later, as turnover approached £1 million, he moved to a 3000 square foot warehouse and a year after that, as his turnover passed the £2 million mark, he moved to larger premises again. In the new premises, Michael is able to undertake manufacturing and assembly work and, since the costs in Great Britain are less than in Scandinavia, he is now able to export products to Norway.

There were two critical elements in Michael's success. The first was the amount of time he spent undertaking market research so that, by the time he came to sell the products, he was assured of a good reception. He had reduced the risk of failure to the very minimum. Second, he knew that it would take some time to build up contacts leading to sales and that in the meantime he would have a very modest cash flow. By operating from home for 18 months Michael was able to develop the business steadily without having to worry about cash flow to cover overhead costs.

What can a new business learn from the experience of people like Michael and Tom? The most important qualities are an ability to spot an opportunity where other people only see a problem. Most people come across opportunities in the course of their work. Some they see for themselves and some are drawn to their attention by customers who say, 'Where can I get . . .?' Most such opportunities are neglected. Tom and Michael make a living out of exploiting them. If you wish to follow up this opportunity then you could start by writing to the British Importers Confederation whose headquarters are at the London Chamber of Commerce, 69 Cannon Street, London EC4N 5AB; 071–248 4444. They publish a *Directory of British Importers* with a Trade Opportunity Supplement which can help you spot gaps in markets of which you have some knowledge.

Jane Halliday – The dressmaker

For the past ten years the market for dress fabrics in Great Britain has been steadily and inexorably declining. There are many reasons for this. One is that dressmaking is not as widely taught in schools as it used to be. Another is that, as people have become more affluent and as mass-produced clothes of reasonable quality have become widely available in chain stores, the economic attractions of home dressmaking have steadily diminished. Over the last five years, the market for knitting yarns has been declining for much the same reasons. During this period, many shops, especially department stores and other large chain stores, have ceased to sell these products.

However, despite this background of decline, there remain many opportunities for small businesses within this market. As observed in Chapter 2, when large companies start to withdraw from the market they frequently leave behind them opportunity gaps which are highly suitable for exploitation by small businesses. Moreover, in the market for dress fabrics and knitting yarns, it is noticeable that the decline has been concentrated in the cheaper, mass-produced segments. The high quality dress fabrics associated with well-known names like Liberty and Viyella have survived and prospered since no mass-produced garments are able to provide the quality and style that these designs have to offer. The same is true in specialised niches in the market for knitting yarns. Thus, while the low-cost, mass-produced products have been in decline, the demand for high quality yarns associated with top class designers like Kaffe Fassett, Kim Hargreaves and Edina Ronay has been growing.

Customers no longer make their own clothes or knit their own sweaters in order to save money. They do so because they can produce top quality, distinctive garments which are not available except occasionally in a few exclusive stores – and then at very high prices indeed. Moreover, hobbies such as knitting have been transformed by modern designers from a harmless way of spending time on the beach to something more akin to a creative activity which is within the ability and means of many ordinary people. A pattern from a contemporary designer is akin to a work of art. For evidence of this you need look no further than the exhibition of Kaffe Fassett's designs at the Victoria and Albert Museum early in 1989.

Finally, as dressmaking skills have declined and become less common, this has led to a very heavy demand for the services of those dressmakers who are prepared to develop their skills to a high order and make them available to others. When my wife Jane asked me, some 15 years ago, whether I would mind if she contributed to the household income by starting a dressmaking business from home, I was pleased and rather startled. She had worked as a nurse and as an air stewardess and had no experience of running a business, though she was a very accomplished home dressmaker. We quickly discovered that, by putting a few advertisements in the windows of local newsagents, she could obtain more customers that she could comfortably handle.

From this experience we learned two valuable lessons. The first is that you must charge an economic price for your service. If you charge too little you will attract customers who want cheap clothes rather than good clothes and these people can be very difficult to satisfy. If you ask an electrician or a plumber to work for you, he will charge £20–£30 an hour and the level of skill offered by a skilled dressmaker is comparable with this. The second lesson we learned was that the dressmaker needs to exercise some influence over her customers' choice of fabric. Jane was frequently troubled by people who bought patterns and fabrics that simply did not go together, leaving her with an impossible task. We concluded that the solution to this problem was to open a dress fabric shop offering a dressmaking service as an extra selling point. Like most young married couples we were short of money and could not afford to lease commercial premises.

We solved this problem by moving to a house situated in a busy high street in Berkhamsted in Hertfordshire. It had sufficient accommodation for ourselves and our two children and we had previously established, by asking the local planning authority, that there would be no objection to our converting our dining room to a shop. We invested about £2000 in sewing equipment and shop fittings and about £10,000 in stock, financing these with a £7000 bank loan (repayable over five years) and an overdraft facility of £5000 to cover seasonal purchases.

We knew that the greatest problem we would have to overcome was our poor trading position since we were situated about 500 yards from the town centre where both our competitors were situated. We did this in three ways. First, we stocked only high quality natural fabrics (wool, cotton, and silk) and concentrated on well-known names like Liberty and Viyella. These products were not available elsewhere in the town. Second, we offered a dressmaking service to people if they bought our fabrics – a facility offered by neither of our competitors. Third, we advertised heavily. In the week before we opened we had 10,000 cards delivered by the GPO household distribution service to local housing estates.

Spinning Jenny, as we called the shop, started to trade in March 1983 and has been profitable since the day it opened. In our first full year we took £42,000 in sales and after six years this had grown to over £72,000. After three years we decided to start selling knitting yarn and we made the mistake of choosing a brand that was firmly placed in the mass market, similar in quality and in its style of patterns to many others that were on sale elsewhere in the town. The experiment was not successful and after a year we discontinued this line and replaced it with a top quality designer orientated brand (Rowan Yarns of Yorkshire) which chooses designers first and then makes the yarns for them – the right way to go about it. Our sales immediately increased dramatically and yarn is now a major component of our sales.

After six years, the business had clearly outgrown our former dining room (which is less than 170 square feet in size) and, when the opportunity presented itself, we moved the business to separate premises of its own in the town centre. We would not have felt able to do this if we had not had the experience of running the business with low overheads from home. This has enabled us to learn a trade of which neither of us had previous experience; to repay the bank loan; and to build up stocks and other assets amounting to over £20,000 to move into the new premises.

Jane and I have learned three valuable lessons from our experience with Spinning Jenny. The first is to research the market carefully, especially if you have no previous experience of it. Before we opened Spinning Jenny we spent a great deal of time talking to suppliers, to similar shops in other towns and to other dressmakers. I found other businesses extremely helpful when we were setting up. Having made it clear to them that we would not be setting up as rivals in their area, we found them all welcoming and only too happy to talk about their businesses. It is better to learn from other people's experience and mistakes than from your own. It is also much cheaper!

Second, we learned that it is essential to sell distinctive products. If we had opened a shop selling products similar to those sold elsewhere in the town (a mistake we made with our first yarn supplier) I don't think we would have lasted very long. Good products, which people will travel to see, are even more important than a good position. Finally, you must charge the right price for your service. If you charge too little you will find yourself working very hard for little reward. You will resent it and you will attract the wrong kind of customer who will not appreciate it.

If you wish to find out more about the fashion industry with a view to entering it yourself then there are several trade journals and trade fairs which will help you. The *Draper's Record* is published weekly and can be ordered through newsagents. It contains news and articles on the clothing business generally. An excellent publication, available by subscription only, is the *Knitting and Haberdashery Review* from 80a South Street, Romford, Essex RM1 1RX; 0708 24112. This is published six times a year.

The Association of Fashion Fabric Distributors organises a Fashion Fabric Fair twice a year (usually held in February and September) details of which are given in the *Draper's Record*. The event is usually held in London, Manchester or Birmingham. At this Fair you will find most of the leading fabric manufacturers, distributors, paper pattern manufacturers, haberdashers and other suppliers to the trade. Finally, you should take the opportunity to visit RD Franks Ltd, of Kent House, Market Place, London W1N 8EJ; 071–636 1244, where you will find a wide variety of books, magazines and other material relating to the fashion industry.

Peter Venes – Computer repairs

Peter Venes is 30. He has many of the characteristics of the typical entrepreneur – resilience, determination and a real enjoyment of his work – though the business he runs is far from typical. Peter left school when he was 16 and attended the local adult education college to qualify in electrical engineering. This he achieved after five years with a mixture of full-time and day-release study. At an early stage in the course he had been taken on by a major computer manufacturer who gave him the opportunity, during the course of his training, to spend short periods in virtually all the company's departments.

After qualifying he became a test engineer – checking that computers were in full working order and ready for sale; and after two years of this he was put into the repair department where he was given the job of repairing components that did not function correctly. It was at this point that he began to learn the intricacies of computer repair work which were to form the basis of his business. Finding his path to promotion blocked on account of his youth (he was six years younger than other people doing similar work) he moved to another company who asked him to set up and run a workshop to repair defective parts from their computers. He did this in London for two years until early 1984 at which time the market for home computers was really beginning to take off.

It is unusual for entrepreneurs to emerge from big companies but at this point, Peter, tired of commuting to London and working the very long hours required to keep the machines running, decided that he, together with two friends, would open a computer shop in the town where they all lived. They put together a business plan which they presented to their local bank manager. Since they were relatively young and unable to offer any security the bank manager said that, though the idea appeared to be sound, he would not be able to advance them the money. However, he referred them to the provisions of the government's Loan Guarantee Scheme (for details see Chapter 9) and, with the assistance of this scheme, they were able to obtain the necessary money and open the shop.

For two years, the shop traded successfully. By a mixture of computer sales together with repair work which was brought to them by other shops and distributors, the partners built up a successful business. However, in 1986 the practice of price cutting became very widespread in home computers. Peter and his partners found that it was impossible to run the business profitably while charging the same prices that could be offered by multiples like Dixons whose bulk purchases enabled them to obtain heavy discounts from suppliers. Peter found it particularly frustrating that he often spent many hours explaining to potential customers the relative advantages and disadvantages of various models for their purchase, only to find that they then made use of his (free) consultancy to purchase the equipment from chain stores. The partners therefore decided to liquidate the shop, paying off all their suppliers and leaving themselves with only £300!

Peter's knowledge of computers is such that he was presented with many opportunities for secure employment with large manufacturers of the kind with whom he had previously worked but it was at this point that his entrepreneurial characteristics began to assert themselves. Most people, faced with a business failure, would have been only too pleased to go back into the security of employment but he was convinced that he had seen an opportunity for running a business based on computer repairs alone. During the last few months of the shop's existence it had been kept going by the profits earned from this part of the business.

Peter used his last £300 to set up a business dedicated solely to this activity. He was unable to qualify for the Enterprise Allowance Scheme because the administrators took the view that his proposed business was too similar to his previous one for him to do so. Nevertheless, he took a lease on a small office and started to contact shops, small manufacturers and distributors of computer equipment. He also advertised in the computer press and in Yellow Pages and in a very short time the work started to arrive. For 18 months he worked alone, collecting and delivering the faulty equipment from shops, offices and warehouses. He had discovered that, whereas there are several organisations who will undertake repair and maintenance contracts for really large companies (eg British Aerospace or British Telecom) there are very few competent organisations who will undertake similar work for companies that have small computer installations. These can range from the small business which may have one desk-top computer on which the business depends for its accounts etc, to others that may have 20 or 30 pieces of equipment.

After 18 months, the business had built up to a point where he needed to engage a secretary/administrator. Six months later he took on a second engineer and 12 months after that a third engineer so, at the end of his third year of trading, Peter now has three people working for him and a turnover of approximately £200,000. Peter believes it is a mistake to look too far ahead in a business in which technology is changing so rapidly and so he is reluctant to predict the directions in which he will want to take the business over the next few years. However, he does believe that the market is becoming more orientated towards replacement rather than repair of components in defective machines. He also believes that, in his own words, 'It's a young industry which is growing very fast.' This is confirmed by the analysis in Chapter 2 indicating that service businesses of this kind are among the most rapidly growing sector of our economy.

Caroline Broon – The hairdresser

Caroline Broon is 20. She left school when she was 16 and took up an apprenticeship at a hairdressers – a job she had wanted to do since the age of five. She completed the City and Guilds Course (a mixture of day release and experience in an established salon) in three years and, after working for a year as a fully trained hairdresser, decided that she would prefer to be her own boss. This is partly because she valued the freedom which this would give her and partly because, as she put it, 'There was more money in it.' She invested about £400 in equipment and took out a loan to buy a reliable second-hand car.

Her first task was to find some customers. It is normal practice in hairdressing that, when a person hands in her notice, she is asked to leave immediately in order to reduce the likelihood of her taking clients with her. In addition, the contract of employment usually specifies that the employee cannot set up in business within about five miles of her place of work. She therefore decided to concentrate on seeking clients in the area close to her home, some five miles distant from her previous place of work. Her main advertising medium consisted of cards in the windows of newsagents – a cheap, cost-effective and greatly underrated medium. Her business built up quickly and, as she became established, word of mouth recommendations led to more customers. When I spoke to her, almost exactly a year after she started, she was earning an average of about £150 a week (for five or six hours a day) compared with the £95 which she had been earning in the salon (working a longer day), so her belief that she would be able to make more money by working for herself has proved to be correct. It should be noted that her earnings can vary from as little as £75 in one week to as much as £200 in another.

Caroline has discovered that the great majority of her customers are women (usually in their thirties) with young children who find it difficult to secure the services of babysitters to look after their children while they are having their hair done in salons. Moreover, this type of customer is likely to be prepared to spend a reasonable amount on having her hair permed, highlighted etc. Some mobile hairdressers make the mistake of concentrating almost exclusively on older clients who are attracted not by the convenience of the service but by its cheapness. This can be critical to the success of the enterprise. One of the main problems confronted by the mobile hairdresser is that of making effective use of her time. A good deal of time is spent travelling and it takes no longer to travel to a customer who wants to spend £20 on a perm than it does to travel the same distance to an elderly lady who wants her hair cut and blow dried for £3 or £4. Moreover, by concentrating on young families, Caroline is also able to pick up business by cutting the hair of the children from time to time at no additional travelling cost.

A major priority for Caroline in managing her time effectively is to ensure that her clients are grouped in such a way that she does not have to travel too far between appointments on any given day. Thus, she will try to arrange the appointments so that she has four or five clients consecutively in one town on a given day. The following day she will visit another town and so on. This occasionally requires some persuasive telephone work but it is essential if she is to make cost-effective use of her time. She may also find it necessary to work as late as 9.30 pm on two or three evenings a week in order to suit her customers.

It is interesting to compare Caroline's experience with that of a mobile hairdresser featured in the video 'Eye for Enterprise' available from the Training Agency (see Chapter 9). In the latter case, the hairdresser found that, while working very hard, she was making very little money because she was spending too much time travelling and paying too much for her hairdressers' supplies – shampoos, setting lotions etc. Caroline has solved the latter problem by buying in bulk from a wholesaler at a fraction of the price that she would have to pay in a chemist shop.

I asked Caroline what were the most important things she had learned during her first year of trading. She told me that the most vital lesson she had learned was that her most valuable asset was her time and that much of her effort was expended in ensuring that she made the best possible use of this. She is thinking of installing a car phone so that she can make appointments while she is out on the road. At present, she has to depend upon customers telephoning her early in the morning (before she leaves at about 8.30) or leaving messages at her home. Second, she had learned that working for herself really could be rewarding whether measured in terms of finance or job satisfaction.

Pauline Crawford – The image consultant

Pauline Crawford took a degree in sociology with statistics at Exeter University before joining Thomson Holidays as a statistician. She soon graduated to the marketing department and, from 1970 to 1976, she was a product manager with responsibility for marketing a range of Thomson Holidays to Mediterranean destinations. In 1976 she left full-time employment to start a family. The next ten years (her children are now aged 10 and 12) were fully occupied with the duties of a housewife and mother but Pauline nevertheless developed a number of small business enterprises during the free time that she had.

Since the age of 11 she had been an enthusiastic dressmaker so she set about designing and making dresses and quilts which she sold through party plans. In 1985 she started a City and Guilds Course in fashion and design, attending a local education college one day a week until she completed the qualification in 1987. At this stage she was intending to develop her dressmaking business and it was for this purpose that she attended a weekend course on fashion and design at the Missenden Abbey residential centre where she heard a speaker on colour analysis. This is a process by which trained counsellors advise clients (mostly women) on the types of make-up and the colours of clothing that are best suited to their skin texture and which will therefore most enhance their personal appearance. She was trained for this work by another colour counsellor who was part of a network organisation and who recruited Pauline into her network for the sale of a range of cosmetics.

However, Pauline had already become much more interested in the application of colour analysis to the choice of clothing than she was in the sale of cosmetics so in 1988, she and a small group of others set up a network of their own specialising in this aspect of the work. She would advise individual clients, on a confidential one-to-one basis, on the choice of colour co-ordinated clothing which would best suit them. Her work attracted a considerable amount of local interest and was featured in newspaper articles but she was also invited to give talks to local women's groups – women's institutes, church groups etc. Interestingly, she was also asked to give talks to a number of men's groups including two Round Table organisations. Most of her clients at this time resulted from these talks and from word of mouth recommendation and at this point she was charging £95 for a full consultation lasting about half a day.

Pauline's husband is a management training consultant and he suggested that her services could be a useful addition to training programmes designed to develop the self-confidence of management staff. She visited a number of training exhibitions and made useful contacts which led to her giving talks to several organisations in this field. She also made a video with a training organisation which brings together trainers and client companies and this has already produced some valuable business. Pauline followed up another contact which led to her being invited to spend a day at the headquarters of a major London bank counselling some of their senior male executives on the contribution which appropriate personal appearance can make to self-confidence and consequently to business effectiveness. For this she earned a fee considerably more than from her private female clients. Another contact whom she met at a seminar led to a further counselling session followed by a guided shopping expedition on which the client spent £1500!

Pauline has decided to concentrate on the business market for her services and, where possible, to offer her advice in conjunction with management training programmes. There are two reasons for this. First, it is more remunerative since companies can see the commercial value of having staff with the right image and self-confidence. Second, she believes that her counselling is more likely to have a lasting effect on someone who sees it as part of his or her career development than upon private individuals who have no such motivation. She has now designed an attractive and professional brochure which she will be mailing out to management development and training organisations inviting them to include sessions on 'appearance skills' in their programmes. She charges a business consultancy fee.

Pauline is quick to emphasise that this has nothing to do with 'power dressing' – a fashionable concept which invites us to believe that the selection of a tie of the right colour (red is greatly favoured for some reason which I do not altogether understand) will impress clients! Pauline believes that appearance skills have more to do with individual personalities and environments than with the arbitrary choice of particular garments or colours. Thus, the appropriate style for a young banker working in the City of London would be regarded as grotesquely inappropriate on a university campus and vice versa. Pauline's programme aims to create self-confidence through the harmonisation of outer appearance with self-image. The interest in her services expressed by large and sophisticated organisations suggests that there exists a real need for a service of this kind.

What are the qualities which have enabled Pauline to develop a business in a field which is still very unusual and underdeveloped? (It is estimated that there are only about 300 people in the UK who are seriously practising colour and style counselling of any kind and hardly any of these have moved into image consultancy in the business sector.) I think there are three reasons.

First, she has an unusual background with a degree in behavioural sciences and a strong personal interest in clothing design. A knowledge of both these subjects is essential for someone who is trying to help people develop a personal appearance which is in tune with their own self-image. Second, her husband is a management training consultant who has many years' experience of dealing with large organisations and his advice has helped her to avoid some elementary mistakes often made by people who are going into the field for the first time. For example, people frequently charge too little for their services, consequently creating an impression that their services are inferior. This would be fatal when dealing with large sophisticated organisations. The prices she charges are realistic and in line with those charged by other consultants. To use her own words 'I've got over the business of apologising about the price.'

Finally, Pauline has a strong personality and the persistence which is required to follow up leads and contacts and turn them into business. She has never spent a penny on advertising and all her clients have come from personal contacts made at seminars, exhibitions and training sessions. She never turns down an opportunity to talk to a group of people even if she is not paid for it since she believes that this is the best way to generate new business. In other words, Pauline is one of nature's entrepreneurs who has a strong belief in what she is doing and the determination to succeed. Some business start-up packages imply that, if you buy their services, the world will deliver a market to your doorstep without your having to go out and find it. If this were true we would all be rich! Pauline has gone and found her market for herself.

If you want to know more about appearance skills counselling write to: Crawford Associates, Winton House, 78 Bois Lane, Chesham Bois, Buckinghamshire HP6 6BJ.

Christine Oxford – The employment agency

Christine Oxford left school at the age of 16 with eight O levels and took a job for the summer as a travel representative with a tour company in Spain. On returning to England she took a job with an employment agency which specialised in recruiting medical staff for its clients. Christine's job was to recruit suitable medical secretaries, occupational therapists, administrative and clerical staff for employment in NHS establishments, general practices and private hospitals. She prepared the advertisements, interviewed the applicants, and matched their qualifications and needs with those of her clients. She described this process to me as 'like assembling a huge and complicated jigsaw puzzle with several pieces missing'. For three months she worked under the supervision of an experienced operator who trained her. At the end of this period her supervisor left and Christine was left with the job of filling her role. She worked seven days a week from 9 in the morning till 9 in the evening for a salary of £54 plus a 1/2 per cent commission on the business she was able to generate. Even in 1980 £54 was not a great deal of money for so much work! However, within 12 months Christine's hard work had earned her a reputation in this specialist field and she was persuaded to join a competitive organisation for whom she worked for 18 months.

After a further 18 months Christine and two colleagues formed a limited company with a view to establishing their own agency. To do this they had to register for VAT and obtain a licence from the Department of Employment as required by the Employment Agency Act 1973. To obtain such a licence it is necessary to persuade the Department of Employment that you are of suitable character and experienced in employment agency work. The Act was introduced to prevent the exploitation of freelance staff by unscrupulous agencies.

The company obtained a loan of £25,000 which was used to secure suitable premises in London and to pay overheads before business started to flow in. Employment agencies are a field in which personal contacts with clients and freelance workers are of paramount importance and Christine and her partners were able to bring with them many of the contacts they had made in their previous jobs.

For the first 12 months Christine and her fellow directors did all the work required. They found the clients; they advertised for, interviewed and recruited the staff required by the clients; they prepared and sent out the invoices and handled the credit control; they answered the phone; they wrote all the letters; they paid all the bills and they cleaned the offices. In the first 12 months they generated a turnover of £750,000 on which their commission was about 15 per cent. At this point Christine and her fellow directors decided that it would be appropriate for them to extend the range of their services to include the recruitment of nursing staff. For this, they had to recruit extra qualified personnel to assist them with the recruitment and selection but this was more than justified by the extra business generated. By 1989 the business was generating a turnover of £6 million and employing 25 full-time staff.

During this period of amazing growth Christine has had to worry about two major problems. First, the administrative capacity of the company simply was not keeping pace with the company's growth. The expertise of the founding directors lay in the fields of advertising, staff interviewing and recruitment and the company's administration tended to be neglected. Consequently, money was not being collected from clients as quickly as it should have been and records were haphazard, making it difficult to prepare the end of year accounts and produce projections of profits and cash flow. Christine and her fellow directors were so busy looking after the customers that the company's finances were being neglected. Finally, an accountant from the company's auditors had to be called in, at considerable expense, to establish a suitable accounting system.

The second problem concerned Christine's fellow directors, who, for personal family reasons, found it necessary to withdraw from active participation in the running of the company. The original Memorandum and Articles of Association under which the company was formed had not made adequate provision for this eventuality. Complex and lengthy negotiations were required to ensure that their withdrawal could take place without causing the company to collapse financially. These proceedings extended over more than a year and took up much of the time and energy of the company's management. The experience has also proved costly since Christine estimates that the company has spent over £100,000 on accountancy and legal fees to deal with these two issues.

By any standards, this is a remarkable story. Christine's business has grown from nothing to a position where it is one of the leading operators in its field within a period of five years. It is well established, respected and profitable. This success must be attributed to the zeal and energy shown by Christine and her colleagues in the early days when they were working with almost unnatural energy. Nevertheless, two salutary lessons have been learned. The first is that administrative and financial controls are neglected at the peril of any company and such neglect can be very expensive to remedy. The second is that complex and expensive problems can result when founders of a company decide to go their separate ways. Even when a company is successful, as Christine's has been, it can run into difficulties because the personal needs and wishes of its founders diverge. At one time, Christine feared that this could bring about the end of the company. The company has survived these difficulties but it would have developed more surely, and with less anxiety to its founders, if some of these problems had been foreseen.

Franchising – Wetherby Training Services

As we saw in Chapter 3, franchising is one of the most rapidly growing sectors in the British economy. It is estimated that annual sales via franchised outlets are growing by about 25 per cent per annum and that between 1988 and 1993 they will further increase from £3.8 to £9.8 billion. Surveys among enterprise agencies also suggest that they are a relatively low-risk method of starting a business. Failure rates among franchised operations in the first years of trading are lower than in non-franchised operations. However, failures do occur and when they happen they can be disastrous for those involved. I am aware of at least one person who invested £17,000 (his bounty on leaving the RAF) in a well-established franchise operation and lost all of it. He made the mistake of going into a franchise covering a business of which he had absolutely no previous experience. He had to learn too much in too short a time. Successful franchisees are often found among people who have previous experience of the business. The case study which follows, covering Wetherby Training Services, features a person who has used the franchise route to establish herself in a business of which she already had some knowledge.

Wetherby Training Services was formed in 1977, specifically to open up franchised secretarial centres using self-teaching or open learning principles. They now have a national franchising network specialising in computer training which today claims to be the largest of its kind in the UK. The flexibility of the training programme gives Wetherby a competitive edge over colleges and other full-time private institutions. It has a special appeal to women planning to return to work after their families have matured, graduates requiring an extra skill and those already in work needing a refresher course and/or updated skills. It appears that, with the demographic changes forecast for the 1990s, qualified secretaries and office workers, especially those with information technology skills, will find their services in great demand. Wetherby hopes to be able to take advantage of this demand.

The Wetherby Training Services Organisation provides audio tuition cassette tapes and comprehensive student workbooks from which the student can follow the course. It is estimated that about 70,000 students are trained each year in this way. The local franchisees operate under their own names, often as part of an employment agency or similar enterprise. They are asked, however, to use a Wetherby corporate logo on all their literature.

Wetherby offers its franchisees a complete package to set up their own secretarial/computer training centres. There are two packages covering everything from workbooks and cassettes to tables and chairs. The smaller package costs £10,500 plus VAT and the larger package £13,700 plus VAT. In both cases, the package includes a franchise fee of £3500. No royalty payments are made by franchisees. Wetherby make their profits from selling the student programmes and workbooks to the centres. They do, however, require an annual licence fee of £350. The franchise fee includes the cost of three days' training which is carried out at Harrogate or another suitable venue and the franchisee has the exclusive right to offer the Wetherby service over a territory which is mutually agreed. The franchisee is required to find suitable premises – between 200 and 600 square feet – as near to a town centre as possible and, as previously indicated, sometimes in association with another related business such as an employment agency. Wetherby mark student test papers and issue certificates of proficiency when the courses are successfully completed. They can also offer Royal Society of Arts and Pitman examinations.

The proprietor of CBA Office Training, which is the Wetherby franchisee in High Wycombe, Buckinghamshire, had some previous experience of this type of work since she was already running an Alfred Marks franchised employment agency. She had been subjected to a very areful selection procedure by Wetherby who are anxious to ensure that ll their franchisees are aware of what they are taking on and sufficiently xperienced and competent to make a success of the operation. As indicated n Chapter 3, franchisors who accept franchisees too readily are to be egarded with caution. She spoke highly of the Wetherby organisation nd was complimentary about the support and advice that was available o her when she needed it. Wetherby forecast a net profit of £ 20,000 efore tax and depreciation, wages and interest payments in year 1 and he franchisee considered this projection to be about right. She emphasised hat the training programmes supplied by Wetherby were very good and ppreciated by students.

It appears that Wetherby Training Services have come up with a good ormula which has expanded steadily over the last ten years to meet a rowing consumer demand in the area of training and new technology. This is a field which, as we saw in Chapter 2, is rapidly expanding and here is every reason to suppose that the need for skilled staff of this ind will continue to grow. Franchising has allowed Wetherby to expand oth in the UK and abroad, giving a guaranteed distribution network or their product while at the same time allowing their franchisees to arn a living from a sound business system, provided, of course, that he franchisee is prepared to work hard and rise to the challenge of elf-employment. The franchise is not suitable, in the opinion of both ranchisor and franchisees, for part-time work as it needs a good deal f commitment. Details of the inventory and capital requirements for the wo Wetherby packages are available from Wetherby Training Services, lockton House, Audby Lane, West Yorkshire LS22 4FD; 0937 63940 nd 63032.

Further Business Opportunities

Dress Hire

One of the most rapidly growing businesses in the service sector is that vhich involves hiring out *special occasion* dresses. They can be cocktail dresses, ballgowns or even wedding dresses. These are all garments vhich are likely to be worn very infrequently, or, in the case of wedding dresses, only once. Consequently, people are very reluctant to invest arge sums of money in buying them and prefer to hire them. Many f the organisations in this business operate from private homes. This nables the proprietors to keep down their overhead costs by avoiding he need to pay rent and it also makes it easier for a busy housewife o combine the task of running the business with running a household. Hire fees range from under £40 to over £100 depending upon the type of dress.

There are many advantages in being a franchisee in this sector – not th least being that buying of garments by franchisors who are in touch wit current fashion trends will reduce both the cost of purchasing the garmen and the likelihood of taking on garments which fail to attract custome because they are the wrong colour, style etc. A further advantage franchising is that it is frequently possible for different franchisees swap garments among themselves if, for example, you are trying to f out a customer who is of an awkward size. Two franchise organisatio operating in this sector are:

Bow Belles Bridal Hire Ltd, Unit 9, Colwick Business Park, Priva Road No 2, Colwick Park, Nottingham NG4 2JR
Just for the Night, 80 Sandridge Road, St Albans, Hertfordshire

Driving Instructor
The number of people taking the driving test continues to increase ye by year, as does the number of instructors required to teach them. Mo people like to take driving lessons in the evenings or at weekends so th is a business which is comparatively easy for an individual to start up conjunction with a regular job. A further advantage is that it involves lo overheads. The only equipment required is a car with dual controls, a advertising headboard and L plates. These can be added to an ordinar car at the cost of few hundred pounds.

Entry to the profession is strictly regulated by the Department Transport. First, you have to become a *Licensed Trainee* which entitles yo to charge for your instruction and involves taking a written and practic examination. After passing these examinations, you have to practise as Licensed Trainee for six months before you can take a final examinato which requires you to give a driving lesson to a senior Departme of Transport Test Examiner. If you pass you become a Departme of Transport *Approved* Driving Instructor. For further details write The Department of Transport (Driving Instructors), 2 Marsham Stree London SW1P 3EB.

Several organisations run courses for potential driving instructors an for details of these you should write to the Driving Instructors Associatio at Lion Green Road, Coulsdon, Surrey CR3 2HL. A full course instruction to cover both parts of the test will cost about £700.

Driving instructors charge from £8 to £15 an hour for their wor depending upon the part of country in which they are located and th local competition. You may decide to take out a franchise from th British School of Motoring who can be contacted at the British Scho of Motoring Ltd, 81–87 Hartfield Road, Wimbledon, London SW19 3T 081–540 8262.

Networking

Networking is a method of selling through a network of personal contacts and is used in the marketing of a wide range of products particularly in the field of toiletries. Broadly, a network operates as follows. If you are recruited into a network and sell products for use by your friends, acquaintances and colleagues, you will be rewarded by receiving commission on the purchases they make – not unlike selling from a Littlewoods catalogue or selling Avon products. Commission on sales of this kind would be in the region of 20 per cent. However, under the networking system the person who recruited *you* to the network also receives commission on the sales you make – though at a lower level, more like 3–10 per cent. Likewise, if you recruit agents who sell to their friends you receive commission on their sales. I have met people who have succeeded in building up large and active networks in this way and who have earned considerable sums of money – tens of thousands of pounds.

However, many network organisations give the impression that recruits can earn large sums of money without requiring much selling ability. This is not the case. To make significant sums of money you have to know a good deal about selling; you must be persistent and active in seeking out recruits to your network; and you must be committed to the product you are offering. It is also helpful to become involved in the network in its early days before the most promising users have been recruited by someone else. For this reason, you should be very cautious of entering into any network until you are sure of your commitment to it. A few people make large sums of money from networking but a much larger number earn very little. Networking is sometimes referred to as multi-level marketing or MLM. You should not become involved in any networking until you have spoken to three or four people already involved in it and have established what your commitments will be and what the true potential earnings are.

Catering

This is one of the most interesting and enjoyable businesses that can be run from home on a flexible basis. Before making food for sale you have to comply with the Food and Drugs Act 1955 and the Food Hygiene Regulations 1970. These require you to register with your local authority's environmental health department who will need to be satisfied that the conditions which apply in your kitchen are suitable. Some businesses cater for a very wide range of clients, while others concentrate on one or two sectors: wedding catering; executive catering; children's parties (often in association with an entertainer); dinner parties; clubs and societies.

Even if you are an enthusiastic and competent amateur cook it is worth enrolling on a course at your local adult education centre in order to learn some of the tricks of the trade – the economics of catering; how to keep food fresh for longer periods than would normally be necessary etc. Such classes can also be very useful contact points since you may meet other people who have complementary skills to your own and these will enable you to undertake a wider variety of tasks.

It is not unusual to find people with businesses, run from ordinary domestic kitchens, turning over £600 – £1000 a week by providing a service to local communities. The film unit of the Shell Oil Company has produced a series of videos about people running their own businesses and one of these features a very successful home-based catering business. If you would like to see the video, contact the film unit at Unit 2, Cornwall Works, Cornwall Avenue, Finchley, London N3 1LD. The video has been produced for educational purposes and is normally loaned to organisations rather than private individuals, but you can borrow it through any college, school, enterprise agency or similar group.

You should also purchase a book called *Running Your Own Catering Business* by Ursula Garner and Judy Ridgway published by Kogan Page at £5.95.

Mail Order Business
There are many books and business start-up packs available which stress the profits which can be made from a mail order business. It is certainly a huge business with sales of £4 billion a year in the UK alone, and some people have made a great deal of money out of it, but some of the business start-up packages understate the problems.

First, it is essential to have the right products to sell. To make a success of a mail order business you need products with a generous gross profit margin to cover the costs of advertising and promoting them. Also, they need to be products which are not readily available by other means. One of the main reasons that people purchase items by mail order is that they believe (often wrongly) that the products are not available in shops. This is one of the reasons that many books are sold by mail order since there are, at any one time, about half a million books in print and only about 5 per cent of these are available in good bookshops.

Second, many mail order operators underestimate the problems of advertising. The rules governing the advertising of products for sale by mail order are very rigorous and it may be difficult to persuade some publications to accept your advertisement unless you have a good track record and can convince the publisher that you will be able to honour any orders which are sent to you by his readers. Moreover, new mail order businesses starting up will have to pay the full rate for advertising in media whereas well-established organisations can purchase advertising space at very hefty discounts, putting them at an advantage over the small operator. Direct mail advertising can be very effective in promoting mail order products but you should not overestimate the response rate. A 2 per cent response rate to direct mail promotion is about average (ie a 98 per cent wastage rate) and 5 per cent is very good indeed. You are unlikely to achieve these levels in the early days.

With all these reservations, mail order can be an attractive and profitable opportunity provided it is thoroughly researched. There are many books on the subject of which one the best is *Running Your Own Mail Order Business* by Malcolm Breckman (Kogan Page, £6.99).

Home Tutoring

This is an opportunity which is well suited to teachers (including retired and semi-retired teachers) and also to non-teachers who have a good knowledge of subjects which are in heavy demand, notably maths. Many retired teachers earn sizeable supplements to their pensions by taking on tutoring work. The lowest rates are for teaching certain arts subjects (eg history, English) in the provinces where about £5 – £8 an hour can be charged for individual tuition. The highest rates of pay are for teaching maths and certain science subjects in and around London where one can earn £11 an hour. Higher rates can be charged for tutoring groups of two or more pupils.

The most cost-effective way of finding potential pupils is to advertise in the local newspaper and also in the windows of newsagents sited close to middle-class housing estates, since it is from areas of this kind that most pupils come. The best time to recruit pupils is in late August/early September (when students are regretting the GCSEs and A levels they have just failed); and in early January when parents are beginning to worry about the examinations the following June.

You may find it helpful to contact Personal Tutors of Cheadle House, Mary Street, Cheadle, Cheshire SK8 1AH who are always on the lookout for people with a degree or teaching certificate to add to their register of people who are prepared to undertake home tutoring. Personal Tutors advertise regularly in local media and, for a small fee, can direct enquiries to local tutors on their register. They also give clear guidance on hourly rates which can be charged for different subjects in different areas.

Conclusion

The purpose of this book has been to suggest ways in which potential entrepreneurs, like yourself, can identify suitable opportunities on which to build a business. I hope I have managed to convince you that many such opportunities exist in manufacturing, retailing, catering and especially in the service sectors for people with the right determination to make use of them. If this book helps you to avoid some of the elementary mistakes and to make a success of one or more of the opportunities it will have served its purpose. Good luck, and if you have time, write and let me know how you are getting on!

Further Reading from Kogan Page

Kogan Page publish an extensive list of books for small and medium-size businesses; those particularly helpful to the reader of this book are likel to be:

Buying and Renovating Houses for Profit, 2nd edn, K Ludman and R Buchanan, 1989

Buying a Shop: The Daily Telegraph Guide, 4th edn, A St J Price, 1989

Buying for Business, Tony Attwood, 1988

The Entrepreneur's Complete Self-Assessment Guide, Douglas A Gray, 198

The Good Franchise Guide, 2nd edn, Tony Attwood and Len Hough, 198

How to Buy a Business: The Daily Telegraph Guide, 2nd edn, Peter Farrel 1989

Law for the Small Business, 6th edn, Patricia Clayton, 1988

Running Your Own Antiques Business, Noël Riley and Godfrey Golzer 1987

Running Your Own Boarding Kennels, Sheila Zabawa, 1985

Running Your Own Building Business, Kim Ludman, 1986

Running Your Own Catering Business, Ursula Garner and Judy Ridgway 1984

Running Your Own Estate Agency, Val Redding, 1988

Running Your Own Hairdressing Salon, Christine Harvey and Hele Steadman, 1986

Running Your Own Mail Order Business, Malcolm Breckman, 1987

Running Your Own Photographic Business, 2nd edn, John Rose and Lind Hankin, 1989

Running Your Own Playgroup or Nursery, Jenny Willison, 1989

Running Your Own Pub, Elven Money, 1985

Running Your Own Restaurant, Diane Hughes and Godfrey Golzen, 198

Running Your Own Shop, 2nd edn, Roger Cox, 1989
Running Your Own Small Hotel, 2nd edn, Joy Lennick, 1989
Running Your Own Smallholding, Richard and Pauline Bambrey, 1989
Running Your Own Typing Service, Doreen Huntley, 1987
Start and Run a Profitable Consultancy, Douglas A Gray, 1989
Starting a Successful Small Business, 2nd edn, M J Morris, 1989
Taking Up a Franchise: The Daily Telegraph Guide, 6th edn, Colin Barrow
    and Godfrey Golzen, 1989

Index